THE WELL-CONNECTED GARDENER

THE WELL-CONNECTED GARDENER

GARDENER

A Biography of Alicia Amherst,
Founder of Garden History

Sue Minter

Book Guild Publishing

Sussex, England

First published in Great Britain in 2010 by
The Book Guild Ltd
Pavilion View
19 New Road
Brighton, BN1 1UF

Typesetting in Garamond by
Norman Tilley Graphics Ltd, Northampton

Printed in Great Britain by
CPI Antony Rowe

A catalogue record for this book is available from
The British Library.

ISBN 978 1 84624 513 8

To M.A.

The journalist who misrepresented my views and, in so doing, inadvertently gave me the opportunity to write this book.

Contents

Acknowledgements

I am indebted to many people in the research for this book. The trustees of Chelsea Physic Garden kindly gave me permission to search Alicia's uncatalogued archive in the library there, and the Curator, Rosie Atkins, arranged access for me.

Elizabeth Orr Sutcliffe was very helpful in showing me her Amherst archive at Didlington Manor, the house she has had built on the site of the original Didlington Hall in Norfolk. Several archivists were very helpful, including the staff at the Norwich County Records Office, the Hackney Records Office, the Women's Library at the London Metropolitan Archive, the Griffith Institute, University of Oxford and the Library at the Royal Botanic Gardens, Kew.

Most of all I would like to thank the Amherst and Cecil families, particularly Oriel Robinson, the Honorable Mrs Angela Reid and Mrs Venetia Chattey, both daughters of Margaret, Alicia's elder sister. The Right Honorable the Lord (James) Rockley gave me excellent access to the library and photograph albums at Lytchett Heath. All of them have been most hospitable.

Finally I would like to thank Ed Ikin who started off the work on Alicia by his MA thesis, Jean Davis and Judy Geffen for arranging accommodation during my researches, Hilary Duckett for expert typing, Penny Hammond for encouragement and Lilian Clayson, whose bequest helped finance the publication. The Stanley Smith (UK) Horticultural Trust kindly helped finance part of the cost of the illustrations.

Sue Minter

Preface

Alicia Amherst is not a well-known name in horticultural history, unlike her near contemporaries, Ellen Willmott and Gertrude Jekyll, though she published far more than the former and as much as the latter. She was honoured in her lifetime – a CBE and then DBE – for her charitable horticultural work, and recognised by both the Worshipful Company of Gardeners as its first female member and as a Citizen of London. She gave us the first comprehensive history of gardening in England (and was the first to draw on manuscript sources), books on children's gardens and the gardens of London, on historic gardens and on the flora of the Commonwealth, yet there is no entry for her in *The Oxford Companion to Gardens*. Why has she been so neglected?

Though all three women were wealthy, both Ellen Willmott (a friend of Alicia's) and Gertrude Jekyll remained unmarried and devoted themselves almost exclusively to their gardens. Alicia, however, had substantial political interests both in her own right and as the wife of a Tory minister. All three women wrote, but Ellen produced but one magnum opus, *The Genus Rosa*, apart from her book of photographs, *Warley Gardens in Spring and Summer*, published by Quaritch. Gertrude wrote mainly in late middle and old age whereas Alicia's authoritative *A History of Gardening in England*, also published by Quaritch, came out when she was but thirty and when Gertrude was primarily known as a jobbing journalist.

The reasons for Alicia's obscurity lie in happenstance – Alicia's archives have been locked away at Chelsea Physic Garden or have remained with her family. Moreover, a spectacular financial ruin made it very difficult for the Amherst family from 1906 onwards. Nevertheless, Alicia's literary contributions – and her support of women in horticulture – deserve exposure and appreciation. Her life's 'intersections' with notable people, ranging from the archaeologist Howard Carter, the physicist Lord Kelvin, the politician Joseph Chamberlain and the colonialist Cecil Rhodes, make fascinating reading. Simply put, she knew everyone – which is why she had visited, and could write about, so many of their gardens and private archives.

Her intellectual rigour, her wide education and social connections led to her laying the standard for today's study of garden history. Yet she was less a designer than a supporter of the practical skill of the horticulturist. This commands less status, then as now. As Reginald Blomfield wrote in *The Formal Garden*: 'Horticulture stands to garden design as much as building stands to architecture.' Perhaps it is this that has led to her comparative obscurity. How ironic in a nation of gardeners.

1

Didlington Hall: Inception of a Gardener, 1865–75

The future author of *A History of Gardening in England* was born on 13th July 1865 to Margaret née Mitford, wife of Lord Amherst of Hackney. She was the fifth of seven sisters. Hackney rents and property were the source of the Amherst's wealth which enabled them to fund a highly privileged lifestyle on a huge estate of 1,500 acres at Didlington Hall, between Brandon and Thetford in Norfolk. The estate was said to have been gifted to the Amhersts by the Crown for helping General Wolfe defeat the French in the battle for Canada. Here it was that Alicia gained her love of gardening, encouraged by being given a section in the park by one of the lakes on the south side of the Hall and with a view of the boathouses. She recalls:

> From the earliest days I had my garden, several little beds designed by the eldest sisters and we all worked together with 'Brownie' a dear old Shetland pony, on which we all learnt to ride, he carried panniers of grass … gradually the care of it devolved more and more on me and I was practically the sole possessor by the time I was eight or nine, and used to plant my pansies and tend my flowers with utmost care. We each had an island of our own in the lake and as we were allowed to go about in boats from an early age we used to work on them … daffodils planted and dead leaves cleared and so on …
>
> My mother used to work in the garden too and I learnt much of my practical gardening and love of flowers from her. With father it was marking and planting of trees, thinning bows [sic] and cutting vistas. From very early days till now, whenever I was at home with him, I used to walk out about the lake or round the courts, altering, planning, cutting or planting …[1]

Didlington Hall was no ordinary garden. Set within the heathland of Norfolk, the estate was seven miles through and took in several villages.

It was crossed with lime avenues first planted in 1689, one of them called 'The Cathedral Walk', and outgrown hedges of Scots pine, planted to provide shelter for game, sheep and herds of Red Poll cattle for which Didlington became famous. The house sat on a terrace and was reflected in huge lakes created under the patronage of Lord Amherst as a kindness to local agricultural labourers in providing paid winter work. The River Wissey was diverted to fill them, and the one closest to the house, being of puddled clay, never dried out and contained a collection of water lilies. The house was approached by a two and a half mile long lime avenue, and the garden was famous for an herbaceous border, half a mile long and twenty feet wide. There was also a fine rose garden, dotted with columnar yews, which abutted a bathing pool with handsome Italianate changing rooms, a yew maze and a rock garden. To the north of the house was the walled kitchen garden with a range of glasshouses on the south-facing wall, including vineries, peach houses and a pineapple house, entered by the original gate to the Manor House of Hackney at Shacklewell. Twelve men worked in the greenhouses and gardens with extra brought in when needed.

Linking the house to the garden were a line of seven statues well over six foot high which must have looked strange to visitors unprepared for Lord and Lady Amherst's interests in Egyptology. They were Sekhmets, seated statues of the Egyptian lioness-headed goddess, in diorite (black granite). These had been acquired by Lord Amherst in 1864–5 from Dr John Lee of Hartwell House, near Aylesbury, a notable collector. He, in turn, had probably acquired them from the British consular representative in Egypt, Henry Salt, in 1833. Alicia knew them as 'basts' or 'paschts' and one was allocated to each of the seven sisters, despite (one hopes not because of) Sekhmet being the mother-goddess of war and strife. These statues must have made an extraordinary sight. Each was seated on a throne with feet together, hands flat upon knees and holding in each left hand an 'ankh' sign, symbolising life. On the head was a solar disc and long wig falling onto the nude upper body, decorated with a broad collar, bracelets and anklets.[2]

It is clear that Didlington Hall was the centre of a near-feudal estate.

> The Hall, which is an old fashioned house in the Italianate style of architecture, is beautifully situated in a finely-wooded park, which is some 1500

acres in extent and contains a magnificent stretch of water, dotted over with picturesque little islands. On the border of the lake, on rising ground, stands a round tower in brick called 'The Castle Cave' from which charming views are obtained of the fine avenues of limes, which are a conspicuous feature of the scenery, and of what is known as 'Birdcage Island', a romantic spot about a hundred yards distant from this point. This lake has a history attached to it which reflects lasting honour on the squire, for it has been twenty-five years in the making, and originated from Mr Amherst's desire to employ the labourers when out of work, during the winter season, when every other source of labour failed, and which has been regularly done.[3]

The estate had four miles of the River Wissey devoted to trout rearing, a duck decoy, a heronry with 170 pairs, and a spectacular quantity of pheasants, partridge, hare, rabbit, wildfowl, snipe and woodcock which led to regular shooting parties, some attended by the Prince of Wales. The lakes also allowed for otter hunting, then quite an acceptable sport.

Alicia had idyllic memories of her childhood at Didlington. Certain aspects of its garden (such as the 'Green Garden' of bamboos and tropical-style foliage plants for which an itemised invoice exists[4]) influenced her when she created her first garden as a married woman:

> When I speak with feeling of Didlington … there is always magic in the word to me. I always felt there was no place in the world as beautiful, no home in the world as happy, no parents as kind, no family more united … The large museum was not built in those days (not until 1885) and the 'playroom' stood where the beginnings of the room is now, at the end of the drawing room, looking onto a large bed full of herbaceous plants with a row of Egyptian 'paschts' facing it – there we had our dolls' house, with its staircase and six rooms, there we painted and were read aloud to – there we carved and modelled in gutta percha, there we cleaned fresh water mussel shells and thought to find pearls. One could hear the sound of the piano and mother's lovely voice coming from the drawing room, her singing is entwined in earliest memories … There was a sort of feudal feeling very strong, with all the old servants about, and the friendly way we knew and loved all the old people …

The 'Seven Sisters' knew that their wealth was linked to their father's Hackney estates. Though in truth the Seven Sisters area of Hackney predated them, they thought of themselves as the second set of 'Seven

Sisters'. Alicia's older sisters were Mary (called May) born 25th April 1857, who eventually inherited the Amherst title; Sybil (Sib) born 21st September 1858; Florence (Flo) born 25th January 1860 and Margaret (Maggie) born 12th August 1864. Her two younger sisters were Geraldine (Cherry) born 2nd May 1867 and Beatrice (Bea) born 27th September 1869. The Amhersts never had a son. This highly feminine domestic atmosphere was also highly cultured. All the daughters were raised by nurses and governesses chosen for their intelligence, an education augmented by an introduction to their father's splendid library.

> 'Geggie' was our nurse, we loved her – and never had anyone else. She took me when I was born and she dressed me for my wedding. Her real name was Margaret MacGregor – I learnt most from her, she was well read and used to say us poems and although she was strict and particular she made our nursery life very happy … such devotion is rare nowadays …
>
> When I was seven in the early spring of 1873, a new governess came, a Mrs Margaret MacArthur, 'Blenks' our nickname, before there had been sweet devoted Miss Wilkinson, 'Marmie' who had been a friend of mother's, a very clever classic scholar, like some medieval saint … Mrs MacArthur won our confidence and showed us at once her delightful cleverness … she used to be reviewing books for *The Saturday Review* or writing amusing articles in the intervals of teaching. She came from Professor E.A. Freeman who was the author of Scotland in his history series for schools – like him a strong radical (she had long ago become a Unionist) … Father used to read aloud to us about all the subjects he was interested in, art, heraldry, Egyptology, archaeology, and so on. There were evenings too with the microscope and magic lantern views of the East and it made learning somehow a part of one's life; the museum and the library and all of our treasures became part of one's self. I know [*sic*] about Fox's 'Martyrs', folio Shakespeare, Tyndale and Wycliffe, etc. from the time I was very small, certainly by the time I was eight. The old books were a delight …[5]

Alicia's early interest in history was a result of her father's library – a fact which she also acknowledges in the introduction to her *A History of Gardening*. Her father, in turn, had been inspired by Sir Andrew Fountaine's library at Narford Hall near Oxborough where he had been born and brought up, son of Mary Fountaine and William George Tyssen Daniel-Tyssen, later Tyssen-Amherst (1801–1855).

The Fountaine's bibliographic and antiquarian interests dated back to Sir Andrew Fountaine, Lord Burghley, friend of Jonathan Swift, which gave Alicia a strong pedigree in these disciplines. Alicia also believed that it was the Tyssen ancestral link which inspired her father to develop a library devoted to the history of printing, which eventually became the most comprehensive in Britain, containing no fewer than ten Tyndale Bibles.

> The Tyssen ancestors came over from Holland at the time of the Protestant persecutions. They came in a ship of their own called 'The Golden Falcon' at the time of Charles I and settled in Philpott Lane in the city. They were one of the founders of the Dutch Church in London in Austen Friars and bought the properties in Hackney and Foulden. One Appolonia by name had married a nephew of Bishop Rolley. Father was very interested in the Tyssen family connection with the printing in Holland of Tyndale's New Testament. When the book was in printed sheets and inquisitors were searching houses … they were concealed in the bed of one of the Tyssen's [sic] who had just had a baby. They did not try to move her and she was actually lying on them … I rather think it is alluded to in 'Fox's Martyrs' as father possessed a copy of Fox's Martyrs and also Tyndale's 'New Testament' … the whole seemed very vivid to us …[6]

This was the atmosphere of erudition in which the sisters were raised.

In later life, particularly in her mid 30s to 40s, Alicia became very involved in issues aimed at healing the rift between town and country. She was active in an advisory role on the Chelsea Physic Garden Management Committee and helped with 'Town and Country' exhibitions and the planting committee for Hampstead Garden Suburb. It is possible to see these interests dawning in her childhood. The Amhersts always had a London house; from 1873 it was 8, Grosvenor Square. Not only was it a social necessity but it was helpful to Lord Amherst, who served as Conservative MP for West Norfolk from this time, and probably far more comfortable than his club, The Athenaeum. At Didlington, Alicia rode horses (particularly a bay called 'Tabby') as did her sisters. In London they would ride in Rotten Row in Hyde Park and in areas where the suburbs had not yet blossomed: 'In London I rode regularly in "The Row" from the time I was seven … I can see now how people looked at Maggie and me on those spirited ponies, my long very fair hair lain down my back touching the ponies or blowing out as we cantered along and we had blue saddle cloths embroidered with our initials. I heard once people saying "here comes the circus". In these days we did not only ride in Hyde Park or Battersea, but out on the Finchley Road at the grass on the side of the road, quite a country feeling and there were ditches we could jump near Wormwood Scrubs ...'[7]

Curiously for a Norfolk man not born on the coast, Alicia's father also loved the sea. In 1874 he commissioned a yacht called *The Dream* and became a member of the Royal Yacht Squadron. The Hackney Archives show the proposals for this yacht with a 24-foot beam, a four-berth 'Ladies Cabin', two other cabins and a small dining room, with additional space for crew. It was to be berthed at Southampton. In 1875, when Alicia was ten, the children spent their first of many summers at Cowes in the Isle of Wight, at Hill House in West Cowes, where they later (in 1886) played with the Empress Eugénie and her nieces. The children loved it when *The Dream* arrived and was launched in May 1876 and they were taken out for the first of many adventures:

> The yachting, as I said, loomed large in our lives. I think it was in 1873, Father bought 'The Dream', a yawl of 184 tons, from old George Bentinck, Member for West Norfolk. She had been designed by Uncle Fountaine ...
>
> Several summers we had a villa at Cowes and stayed there with Granny while the elder sisters yachted with Father and Mother, and great was our joy when 'The Dream' came to Cowes and we spent most of our time on board.
>
> The nearest way to the beach to Hill House, where we lived, was through the Castle gardens. We had a perfect right to walk through and I am afraid we were amused to see the smart ladies, 'Professional Beauties', looking at us angrily, until one day the Prince of Wales called us – with our buckets and spades – out to him. He had stayed at home, so we were not the least afraid. We made our curtsey, and answered all his questions, as to where 'The Dream' was, and when Father was coming to Cowes. After that the smart ladies used to smile at us.
>
> The only cloud in those happy days at Cowes with Granny was for 2 years caused by the presence of Mademoiselle, our French governess. I don't know why she took a dislike to me; she was the only person I remember being unkind to me. She had canaries in cages, and, what we thought was dreadful, a robin. We knew Blake's lines: 'A robin in a cage puts all heaven in a rage'. We were fond of 'Bobby' and were very sorry for him. One day she asked Maggie to bring her a pailful of sand for Bobby. Maggie forgot and I ran back, quite a long way, to fetch the sand she wanted. She

seized my pail, threw out the sand and said fiercely: 'He shall not have it, you will poison my Bobby.' The injustice of this accusation rankled in my mind for years. All was happiness in the schoolroom after she left and our beloved Miss MacArthur, whom we called 'Blenks' remained for 12 years our only teacher.[8]

The entire Amherst family were very keen on travelling abroad, an interest Alicia retained all her life. It was, however, perhaps because of her experience at the age of six that she feared travelling would always be accompanied by serious health issues:

My first recollections of going abroad were in the early spring of 1872. Our rooms in the Hotel du Louvre, opposite the burnt and ruined Tuileries, as it had been left by the Commune. It frightened us very much. We were taken to the Jardin des Plantes by steamer. That, too, was a great disappointment, as all the animals had been eaten during the siege. Travelling was much more uncomfortable. In this journey, in 1872, we crossed from Folkestone – where we had stayed the night – to Boulogne. The boat was a small paddle-steamer. I think it was rather rough, as a sailor lifted me up on to the narrow seat which ran along the bulwark and covered me over with a tarpaulin. I clung to my doll and enjoyed the splashes. We were an immense party – fifteen in all. Father, Mother and Granny, seven of us, May, Sib, Flo, Magsie, me, Cherry and Bee, the youngest who was two and a half. Miss Gay, the governess, Geggie, the Nannie, Jennie, the nurserymaid, William, Father's valet and Mrs Moore, Granny's maid. After Paris, we were a month at Fontainebleau, as Father and Mother had to return for some business settlement of Mother's Mitford property.

The June we spent at Chaumont, in the Jura, which I think, must be nice and healthy, but I am appalled when I think what we went through at Thun, our next long stop. It sounded charming, a large chalet in the grounds of a hotel which we had to ourselves. The sanitary arrangements were ghastly. I can remember crying when I had to face the smell. Father got a poisoned leg, Cherry got dysentery and May diphtheria. When she was really ill, the rest of us were sent to the Hotel Pension with strict instructions to keep out of the way of two poor children with whooping cough. However, we all survived, and we, little ones, had a happy time on the Lake of Geneva, while the elder ones went mountaineering to Zermatt.

The homecoming was delayed till late in November, as all the cottage children at Didlington had scarlet fever and we were left at Boulogne with Granny.

The long journeys, with all of us children, must have been trying, as there were no conveniences on the trains and no dining cars or sleepers. Sometimes there was a 20 minute stop for a meal at a station, but, of course, for us children, that was no use. I don't think there was much improvement in the trains till the eighties, during which time, we made many journeys.[9]

In 1877, the family had a bout of scarlet fever and limited their holidays on the yacht to Torquay. Alicia went on some longer cruises to Fowey and Plymouth and stayed on board for some weeks.[10]

Alicia was to lose her youngest sister, Bea, to typhoid fever at Cannes on 20th November 1881 when Bea was only twelve. She was the only one of the seven sisters not to survive into adulthood. Later, Alicia was in a position to influence standards on the trains she had so criticised earlier, as her husband became a leading investor in railways and had an interest as an MP in legislation concerning them. Her second to last book, published in 1935, *Wild Flowers of the Great Dominions of the British Empire*, was researched by train.

Alicia's early years confirmed her as a gardener with a strong intellectual bent.[11] It introduced her to the Amhersts' love of antiquarian books and connected her with Egyptology, both of which were to become crucial when she was given the opportunity to write *A History of Gardening in England*. Although her upbringing was highly privileged, it introduced her to the idea that to whom much is given, much is also expected. These themes developed as she progressed through her teenage years and as politics became more of an influence in her young life.

2

*A Learned, Charitable, Travelling, and
Increasingly Political Life, 1875–90*

Didlington Hall, Alicia's home, dated from the seventeenth century but
had been repeatedly extended and was refaced by Norman Shaw RA in
1884 when she was nineteen. A large, Italianate water tower dominated
the skyline and the south front, with drawing room behind, was terraced
down to the lakes. There was also a ballroom, with a famously sprung
floor, and later conservatory which made a frontage of over 250 feet.
Along this were placed the seven Sekhmet figures. Behind the house, the
stable yard had a flint archway which Landseer painted in the background to his picture *The Return from Hawking*. Here also stood the
church of St Michael and All Angels and, further back still, the kitchen
garden.

The house contained the famous and valuable library of books
collected by Lord Amherst in order to demonstrate the development
of printing from earliest Mesopotamian examples, including papyri,
through to the late nineteenth century. Among these were a fine collection of early English herbals and works on gardening, which were the
direct inspiration for Alicia's *A History of Gardening*. She acknowledges
this in the dedication of the third edition (1910) to her father: 'Nearly
all the rare gardening works quoted … were very familiar friends from
my childhood in the "Amherst Library" … I learnt how to read the
cramped handwriting and abbreviations of the old records I had to
consult by practising on … fourteenth-century manuscripts, to which I
had free access at my home. This book is directly the result of living
with these precious volumes, which were collected with great knowledge, and treasured with deep appreciation by my father.' Lord Amherst
was a member of the Society of Antiquaries, a fact which later became

important in launching Alicia as an author. His earliest works were a Block Book of 1430, a Gutenberg Bible of 1455, the earliest printed book bearing a date (a Fust and Schoeffer Psalter of 1457), foreign incunabula including the first book printed in Italy in 1465, the first in Rome (1467), the first with copper-plate engravings (1477), and so on. There were several Caxton Bibles dating from 1474 and a collection of works of the early Norwich press, 1568–1579. To these were added a first folio of Shakespeare. Of papyri, the Amherst collection included the first five verses of Genesis in Greek in a papyrus found at Fayum, dating from the 3rd to 4th century AD and supposedly the first authority for the Bible. Others contained the Book of Job, the Psalms and the Acts of the Apostles; there was also a 10th century Greek manuscript of the Gospels of Luke and John, and Hebrew rolls of the Pentateuch and the Book of Esther. There was a Wyclif *New Testament* from around 1390, Tyndale's *New Testament* of 1534, Coverdale's *Bible* of 1535, Cromwell's *Great Bible* (1539) as well as Cranmer's, Charles I's, and that on which George III took his Coronation Oath; also a first edition of Foxe's *Book of Martyrs*. Illuminated books of hours and missals added to the visual beauty of the collection, as did examples of the best work of book binders.

This extraordinary collection influenced the course of Alicia's life in other ways too. The 'Amherst Papyri' attracted Egyptologists to Didlington, including Percy Newberry who instigated the project which Alicia later developed into the *History*. As well as being an antiquarian, Lord Amherst was very forward looking, and in 1882, Didlington Hall was the first house in the county to have electric light. His library also contained examples of the introduction and spread of rail travel in Britain; especially important were early editions of Bradshaw's *Companion*. Alicia was to do most of her later botanical exploration in the Colonies by rail, and her future husband was to be involved in railway conferences and legislation, and derived much of his income from rail shares.

The house introduced Alicia to the history of the family. There were two branches, each descended from a different son of Thomas Amherst of Amherst, Kent, c. 1489 – the Hackney/Norfolk branch and the Kent branch. In the garden entrance, off the Octagon Room, was displayed the early eighteenth century Amherst Staffordshire china made from designs sent to England by the second Baron and first Earl Amherst in

1820, during his embassy to China (1816–1822). This came from the Kent branch of the Amhersts, Lady Sarah Amherst being the namesake of *Amherstia nobilis,* the tropical tree known as 'The Pride of Burma', and of the showy Lady Amherst's pheasant. Limoges, Majolica and Dresden china adorned the Red Drawing Room, no doubt brought back from Grand Tours, as all the Amhersts were very well travelled. There were portraits everywhere.

In addition, the house had two museums, the Old Museum and the Large Museum, the latter added in 1885, and entered off the Octagon Room. It was 90 feet by 28 feet and hung with Gobelins tapestries of scenes featuring Louis XIV, along with chairs and sofas with similar work portraying scenes from Aesop's fables. The contents included items of local archaeology, weapons and ethnographical artefacts from Nigeria, Sudan, Samoa, Tonga, the Torres Straits and the Solomon Islands. Lord Amherst's interest here derived from his work for the Hakluyt Society: he had translated the accounts of the discovery of the Solomon Islands. There were 2,000 years' worth of cuneiform tablets from earliest Babylonia and from 668 BC to 193 BC – relevant to Lord Amherst's interest in writing as well as printing. With the papyri, terra-cotta seals and other inscribed objects, these 'carry down the history of writing for some three thousand years'.[1]

It was natural that growing up among such a collection should inspire in Alicia a love of history, writing, printing and a curiosity about travel. It set the scene for a number of later achievements. Even the collection of ivory and wood turning (an activity carried on in the upper west wing) may have played a part in creating a precedent within the City livery companies for it had gained Lady Amherst her membership of the Worshipful Company of Turners, and Alicia subsequently became the first woman to be given the Freedom of the Gardeners' Company in 1896, following the publication of the *History*. She described this as 'an honour which for some years I was the only lady to possess, and of which I am extremely proud'.[2] It was, indeed, a very early recognition of Alicia's importance in horticulture. Ellen Willmott (1858–1934) and Gertrude Jekyll (1843–1932), both her near contemporaries (and Miss Willmott a friend), were not awarded the Victoria Medal of Honour by the Royal Horticultural Society until a year later, 1897, the first year it was awarded.

However, the collection which above all else inspired Alicia to travel was the Egyptian, which became the finest collection in Britain in private hands. It spanned both Old and Large Museums and contained stelae and inscribed stones, portrait busts of the Ptolemaic period and a collection of mummy cases (which apparently led to the Amhersts having difficulty retaining domestic servants prepared to dust in the museum!). One of these was of Amenhotep I and contained the body. Another was the first mummy case ever brought to England (1730), others were Ethiopian and Roman, or Graeco-Roman, and had facial portraits in wax. There were mummified cats, crocodiles, ibises and hawks (which must have inspired Lady Amherst in her hobby of taxidermy). There were Shabti figures (which accompanied the dead), plus bronzes of Isis, Osiris and Horus. One of the wooden Shabti with a charming expression was said to have led the Norfolk novelist Henry Rider Haggard, author of *King Solomon's Mines*, to write the novel *She*. The collection also inspired a little-known nineteen-year-old from nearby Swaffham who was a good draughtsman and possibly distantly related to the Amhersts. Both he and his older brother, Vernet, were lined up to provide drawings for Alicia's *History*. His name was Howard Carter and, under the patronage of the Amhersts, he became the most famous archaeologist in history.

The fact that Lord Amherst was an antiquary, a collector, and had a busy life as an MP did not prevent him, or his family, from involvement in other charitable activities. Such philanthropy was expected of 'the quality' and the Amhersts never fell short. He built and endowed five schools on the Didlington estate and funded an Exhibition worth £25 in both 1891 and 1900 to the Gardeners' Company, to be awarded on the results of the Royal Horticultural Society's exams.[3] Some of Alicia's horticultural notes were written on the back of candidature papers for the Eastern Counties Asylum for Idiots and Imbeciles, Essex Hall, Colchester. Poignantly, these were in favour of one Fanny Rose Matthews, born 18th July 1875, daughter of W. Matthews of Watton, Norfolk, the third of seven children, crippled, deaf and poor. She was recommended for admission by Lord Amherst and three others, Alicia being listed as one of two to whom proxy votes could be sent. One wonders what happened to Fanny and whether she improved as they hoped.[4]

The sisters were all keen on painting miniatures, an activity which also spilled over into charity:

[I refer to] the smaller interests, such as the Queen's Hospital for children, which we were taken to when we were quite small and for years supported a cot by our painting. At one time we made cartridge cases, into match boxes, painted. They were sold by Stockley, in Bond Street, for quite a lot. We thought he paid us well and he used to send us quite large orders for hunting and shooting scenes, as well as just dainty designs. But it got almost more than we could undertake when a photograph of a football team was sent to be copied in colours on an eight bore cartridge. Sib did it marvellously, but we all said: Never again! Up till the very end of my active life, I have been down at least once a year to the hospital and helped to raise £1,000 yearly. Princess Beatrice was always to the fore in helping.[5]

Amid all the charitable work, the Amhersts continued to travel and Alicia grew up loving her opportunities to sail on *The Dream*. Not all journeys were uneventful but they introduced her to different cultures. One trip, in the 1870s, was to Norway with her father, May and Flo:

… we were becalmed on the Dogger Bank among the fisher folk and were caught in a sudden storm and it carried away our gaff. I think it was a pretty nasty thing to happen. I believe it was a very bad night and, although our boats were on deck, we nearly lost one of them. William Boddy, who was keeper at home and Steward on the yacht, tucked me up in my berth. By the dim, swinging candle, I read my evening Psalm and, when I got to the verse: 'The waves of the sea are mighty and rage horribly but yet the Lord who dwelleth on high is mightier,' I blew out my candle and slept soundly. The scent of pine trees was strong next morning before we could see the coast of Norway and got into Christiansand. There, I delighted in the wooden houses and primitive carts drawn by ponies with blue reins and bells. We went in and out Fjords to what is now Oslo, then down the Swedish coast to Copenhagen. The town was *en fête*, as the Tsar and the Princess of Wales were there.[6]

When she was thirteen, in 1878, they went to Paris to see the Exhibition and she revealed her interest in developing technologies: 'In the Hotel Continental there was a large electric light, a spluttering, dazzling arc light, before incandescent lights were invented. This was thought very wonderful.'[7] They travelled south to the Puy de Dôme and on to

13

Nîmes, noting the gorges and basalt rocks, and then on to spend the winter at Cannes.

> [Here] I had my first thrill of seeing grey olives and blue sea and began my collection of wild flowers. The yacht, 'Dream', had already become part of our lives and, in the spring, she came out to Cannes. Sib, Flo and Maggie had gone to Florence and Rome and the rest of us went along the Riviera, in the yacht, all the way to Leghorn, an unforgettable experience. As we flew a White Ensign, at Onelia, the townspeople thought some great personage must be on board. Queen Victoria happened to be at Baveno. When Mother went on shore, they took it into their heads that the Queen had come to Onelia. We were mobbed in the town, crowds following us, and had to take refuge in a shop till the mistake was explained.
>
> We all went to Florence in May. Father, May and Flo joining the yacht, eventually came home round Spain in her, while we returned to Cannes and spent a lovely summer in the Pyrenees. During that winter at Cannes, we went on board the French flagship, when their fleet was in Golfe Juan. 'The Niger' I think; she was an ironclad with steam and sails. While we were on board, we heard the order given 'La Majorité en l'air pour serrer les voiles'. The sails were all hanging out to dry.

Yet illness continued to dog the family. At Bagnières de Bigorre, the children spent seven weeks with whooping cough. Alicia remembered making friends with an old lady, over eighty, whose parents had been guillotined. She also remembered riding and driving in the mountains. This passion for place, for history, for new things, was also matched by an instinct for natural history. She was always collecting and pressing flowers. In spring 1873, when 8, Grosvenor Square became their London home, Alicia was first taken to the Royal Botanic Gardens at Kew by her parents, who knew Sir Joseph Hooker. He '… lifted me up to stand on one of the large leaves of the *Victoria Regina* water lily in the tank', she records.[8] Alicia's elder sisters started attending lectures at the Royal Institution and Alicia soon followed.

She attended many courses of botanical lectures, and a course on Indigestion by Professor Gamjee. She remembered Marconi first demonstrating the transmission of morse code by wireless telegraphy:

> Father was keen on all to do with electricity, so it was mainly to hear Professor Tyndale and Professor Dewar. I was at the Friday evening lecture when Marconi first demonstrated his discovery. The wireless apparatus was

in the basement and he said that he would send a message in Morse into the theatre which the audience could see by a moving light. There was breathless silence; then, suddenly, the Morse began to move. The whole circle of learned scientists were wildly excited – some rushing from their seats to seize Marconi's hand.[9]

As well as having an interest in science and new technological developments, the Amhersts were a highly musical family.

We always had a great deal of music, not only being taken to concerts and operas regularly, but a great deal of really good music at our own house, 8 Grosvenor Square – My mother had a most beautiful, high, soprano voice, and professionals liked to come and play for her and accompany her. Her Master was Garcia, who was a very celebrated singer, who lived to be over 100. Mother was one of his few early pupils who wrote to congratulate him on his 100th birthday. Later her teacher was Maras – he even tried my voice when he was a very old man at Nice.[10]

Later, Alicia (in common with Ellen Willmott) became a member of the Bach Choir. True to his collecting interests, her father had acquired several fine violins including 'a very fine Stradivarius, a Gaspar de Sala, two Amatis and a Guernarius' [*sic*]. This attracted musicians to the house. Alicia remembered attending piano recitals by Hallé in St James's Hall and the poet Robert Browning 'always sitting in the front row'.[11] Many musicians performed at Grosvenor Square and Alicia called it 'wonderful to have such an opportunity of hearing good music before the days of wireless and gramophones.'[12] And, as at Grosvenor Square, so at Didlington, where there was a stage. Lady Amherst was wont to mount operatic parties in the summer with 'opera scenes complete', including on one occasion *The Flying Dutchman*. The sisters sang the choruses.

In the mid 1880s a botanical event occurred which made a deep impression on Alicia. She describes it thus:

I think it must have been in 1883 or 1884, that a plant of the Amherstia Nobilis [*sic*] was sent back to Kew. They had one for a specimen and could not give it proper space, so it was offered to my Father. He, at once, built on a hot house to the existing stove. He made two tanks in which we planted some blue water lilies which had been given to my grandmother and Stocking, the old gardener, had kept alive in a tiny aquarium for forty years. They at once grew and flowered beautifully. The Amherstia was planted in the centre of the house with hot pipes in water all round it, and it had a double glass roof. The Amherstia was evidently quite at home with us, as it grew beautifully and produced lovely flowers in 1887, the Queen's Jubilee. This was specially lucky, as the tree had first flowered in England in Mrs Lawrence's garden in 1837. The tree was discovered in Burma, growing by an old monastery, by Wallich, the botanist at Calcutta, in 1827. I do not think that even yet it has ever been found wild. It was called Amherstia after the second Lord Amherst, who was Governor General of India.[13]

Amherstia is a tropical tree of the pea family with pendant racemes of scarlet flowers. It has the habit common in the tropics of producing its leaves in pendant, soft sheaves and is one of the most spectacular sights in botanic gardens. It is slow-growing and requires very high temperatures and humidity, so no doubt the double-glazing in the Didlington greenhouse helped. Pictures and plans of the glasshouses in the kitchen garden show the long south-facing range with a glasshouse emerging in the centre at an angle of ninety degrees. Between it and the main range was the 'special plant' house, which was also higher. Alicia painted the racemes of *Amherstia* in oils and also photographed it – she was, like Ellen Willmott, a keen photographer and developed her own prints. She was aware of the significance of this plant and later recommended her son, Robert, to read up on its history '… as it was to house the Amherstia that Paxton made the large greenhouse at Chatsworth which led to his being entrusted with the design of the Great Exhibition in 1851'.[14]

In the 1890s Alicia continued to travel with her family, particularly in Europe. She took all her horticultural and botanical interests with her and was always keenly observant. In the Vosges in September 1891 she spent a month noting the flowers and local customs: 'The Vosgeois have a curious way of carting their hay. As soon as it is dry it is tied up in sacking in bundles, and these bags of hay look like huge Mushrooms as they lie in the fields waiting to be carted by the picturesque peasants in their white caps and blue blouses and the patient cream-coloured oxen.' She showed an awareness of the uses to which plants could be put, noting in the fertile Val d'Ajol, its cherry orchards and kirsch distilleries. At Ballon she saw *Gentiana lutea* '… used there for making a strong liqueur ('gentiane'), supposed to be a very wholesome tonic'.[15] This interest in plant usage remained with her all her life.

As well as her horticultural interests, Alicia developed as a political 'animal' from her early teens and she was later to comment to her children: 'All one's life one has been very mixed up with politics.'[16] Canvassing obviously made a deep impression on her:

I was 14 when Father first stood for West Norfolk. He got in at the end of Beaconsfield's administration, at a by-election, and was the last of the jingos. We used to ride about seeing the farmers – going miles into the fen-country. It seems so comic now, the absolute ignorance of what a vote was, and how the older people expected to be bribed. It was in canvassing at Downham Market that I met an old man who had been in Napoleon's *Grande Armée* in the Retreat from Moscow. He was a Pole who had been made to fight with the French. He talked about the awful suffering of the Retreat, especially at one river, where most of them perished. He got back to France and was eventually taken prisoner by the English and remained in England after Waterloo. He asked me questions of what Paris was like then.[17]

Several of the sisters helped with canvassing and did not always have an easy time, especially in bad weather. In the winter of 1888–9 Alicia and sister Cherry got lost in the snow during a blizzard. Having left Downham Market in early afternoon, they finally arrived at Didlington at 11.00p.m. Great anxiety and large chilblains were the result.[18]

Alicia was eventually to marry into one of Britain's most famous political dynasties, the Cecils. Her early awareness of political issues informed her later views, particularly on the Colonies and Women's Suffrage. From 1894 onwards she was deeply involved in the foundation of the Primrose League – an organisation set up to promote Conservative principles and support the Empire, following the example of Benjamin Disraeli – and in 1901 she became a founder committee member of Lady Jersey's Victoria League.

3

Egypt, Percy Newberry and the Howard Carter Connection, 1890–5

The Amhersts' interest in Egypt descended, in part, from Alicia's mother who had, in turn, been inspired by her own father and their first visit to Egypt in 1860: 'In the days of my childhood I listened with breathless interest to the stories told me by my father, the late Admiral Mitford, of Muhammed Ali, with whom he spent some time as a young man; of the journey he took with Ibrahim Pasha; of the beauties of the Nile, and the fairy-like description of Cairo and its inhabitants.'[1]

Perhaps because she had been inspired as a child, Alicia's mother wrote regularly in *Children*, a quarterly magazine for the young priced at sixpence. Sometimes these articles were illustrated by some of her own children, including Mags, and they formed a series. For example, in January 1897 she wrote a story set in 1400 BC.[2] All the sisters became impassioned about Egypt, their enthusiasm leading to a family visit in 1894–5.

In the 1860s Lord Amherst had purchased an Egyptian collection belonging to the Revd R.T. Leider and Dr John Lee, the antiquarian.[3] His interests also led to his becoming a member of the committee of the Egypt Exploration Fund, a body founded in 1882 to promote archaeological excavation in Egypt and publish the results annually for subscribers and (at a price) the general public. Two notable men associated with this organisation were Percy Newberry (1869–1949), a young Egyptologist with an interest in botany and garden history, and William Flinders Petrie who became one of its main excavators.

Percy Newberry, who was four years Alicia's junior, became crucial in the genesis of her *History*. His visits to Didlington in his early twenties probably resulted initially from his links with the Fund and occurred around 1890. This date was important because it coincided with the establishment of an Archaeological Survey department of the Fund, dedicated to recording their excavations for science before the weather and grave robbers had done their work. This required skill in drawing and/or taking impressions, and led Newberry to make an important recommendation.

Lord Amherst's family were interested in sketching and drawing of all kinds. Among their acquaintances were Samuel John Carter of Swaffham and his artistic family – Samuel, Vernet, William, Amy and, significantly, the youngest, Howard Carter. Samuel John painted at Didlington for the Royal Academy Summer Exhibition of 1859 – a falconer's lunch and an infant group. Howard probably visited with his father and seems to have been engaged to catalogue the Amherst collection between 1892 and 1898.[4] There also seems to be a possible family connection with the Amhersts – a 'John Carter of Northwold' married a Mary Ann Daniel Tysson at Foulden in 1819.[5]

Alicia's mother seems to have recommended Howard to assist Newberry on the new Archaeological Survey because of his sketching skills, and on 29th May 1891 she wrote to him: 'I am so glad that you have been able to get an appointment for Howard Carter. I am very grateful to you and I hope he will prove a useful help in many ways … It is a good start to get £100 a year.'[6] Carter had no archaeological knowledge, though his interest had been stirred by the Didlington collection. Lord Amherst therefore arranged for him to work under, and be trained by, Flinders Petrie, an arrangement not entirely without self-interest, as Lord Amherst admitted to Newberry: 'You are quite right that I wished to help Mr Petrie in the excavation and to get if I could some fresh monuments for my museum … if you will kindly arrange that Howard Carter should work for me under him I shall be much obliged.' By 23rd December 1891 he had heard that Newberry had concluded the negotiation and cabled back: 'I accept Petrie's offer let Howard Carter commence under him Tyssen Amherst.'[7]

Carter was seventeen and a half years of age when he joined Petrie on 2nd January 1892 at El-Amarna, where Petrie assigned a special area to him as part of Newberry's team. Petrie's fee was £200.[8] In later life, Carter, by then famous as the discoverer of the tomb of Tutankhamen, admitted his debt to the Amhersts: 'It is to Lord and Lady Amherst that

bove: An aerial view of Didlington Hall between Brandon and Thetford in Norfolk,
icia's childhood home and where she developed her love of gardening.
urtesy of Elizabeth Orr Sutcliffe.

from a drawing in Crayons by Armstrong

SIR. ANDREW FOUNTAIN, KNt.

OF NARFORD HALL, NORFOLK, WARDEN OF THE MINT. OBt. 1753.

Left: Sir Andrew Fountaine of Narford Hall, Norfolk by William Camden Edwards; after Armstrong. Alicia's father was born and brought up at Narford and was inspired to become a bibliophile by Sir Andrew's library. *Copyright: National Portrait Gallery, London.*

Left: Lord Amherst of Hackney, Alicia's father, photographed with a grandchild, probably between 1898 and 1904, Alicia's childbearing years. *Courtesy of Elizabeth Orr Sutcliffe.*

Above: The library at Didlington Hall from the sale catalogue of 1910. It was her father's library (including its old herbals) which inspired Alicia's interest in garden history.
Courtesy of Lord Rockley.

Below: The saloon at Didlington Hall, hung with Gobelins tapestries.
Courtesy of Elizabeth Orr Sutcliffe.

Above: The South Front of Didlington Hall reflected in one of the
many lakes, with the museum below the Italianate tower.
Courtesy of Lord Rockley.

Below: The seven Egyptian 'Sekhmet' figures ranged along the museum frontage, a testament to Lord
Amherst's passion for Egyptology and one dedicated to each of his seven daughters. Alicia was the fifth.
Courtesy of Elizabeth Orr Sutcliffe.

Left: Alicia's photograph of the rare Burmese tree *Amherstia nobilis* taken in 1887, when it flowered in the special tropical greenhouse in Didlington Hall's kitchen garden. Alicia painted the 'family tree' in oils and noted below this photograph 'Father sent a flower to the Queen'. *Courtesy of Lord Rockley.*

Below: Alicia on 'Esau', probably taken during the Egyptian trip of 1894-5, during which she was working on the illustration proofs for *A History of Gardening in England. Courtesy of Lord Rockley.*

Left: The title page of the catalogue of the Society of Gardeners, 1730 - an illustration from *A History of Gardening in England.* Alicia was to become the first woman to receive the Freedom of the Gardeners' Company in 1896 following the publication of her *History...*

Left: Frances Evelyn ('Daisy') Greville (née Maynard), Countess of Warwick, society beauty, mistress of King Edward VII, and founder of the Lady Warwick Hostel for horticultural training for ladies at Reading which became Studley College in 1910. Alicia was a hostel patron and vigorously supported women in horticultural careers. Photograph by Lafayette.
Copyright: National Portrait Gallery, London.

Above: A stern-looking Alicia with husband Evelyn, son Robert, daughter Margaret and the Archbishop of York after Robert's confirmation on 30th July 1916. The Amhersts came from a strong Dutch Protestant heritage. *Courtesy of Lord Rockley.*

Below: Alicia with her younger daughter Maud and granddaughter Juliet, March 1929. Alicia's book *Children and Gardens* of 1903 was partly inspired by having her own children. *Courtesy of Lord Rockley.*

Left: During the First World War, Alicia and two of her sisters worked as nurses in the Red Cross/St John's Voluntary Aid Detachment hospital at Buckenham Tofts Hall, Mundford, Norfolk.
Courtesy of Lord Rockley.

Left: Sir (Lewis) Amherst Selby-Bigge, Ist Bt. by Bassano – 'Doddles' to Alicia. He redirected Alicia from nursing to urgent food production work as 'Honorary Assistant Director of Horticulture' for the war effort in January 1917.
Copyright: National Portrait Gallery, London.

Above: Encouraging Britain to feed itself was crucial in the later stages of the Great War. Alicia encourages the allotment potato harvest, September 1917. She also remembered being photographed spraying potatoes in Hyde Park. *Courtesy of Lord Rockley.*

Left: An undated passport photograph. Alicia had been a worldwide traveller since youth and having a passport was a crucial requisite for her charitable work on emigration. *Courtesy of Lord Rockley.*

Left: Alicia's passport photograph of August 1929. Foreign travel resulted in the publication of *Wild Flowers of the Great Dominions of the British Empire* in 1935. *Courtesy of Lord Rockley.*

Left: Alicia's passport photograph of July 1934. *Courtesy of Lord Rockley.*

Left: Alicia with her granddaughter Oriel
at Lytchett Heath, October 1938.
Courtesy of Lord Rockley.

Below: Lytchett Heath, near Poole in Dorset,
Alicia's country home from 1921 until her death.
She remodelled the garden's terraces - compare
with Alicia's watercolour (colour picture 15).
Courtesy of Lord Rockley.

Left: Lord Eustace Cecil, Alicia's father-in-law and creator of Lytchett Heath and its gardens, 1911. *Courtesy of Lord Rockley.*

Below: Alicia and Evelyn with their children Margaret (left), Robert and Maud, photographed at Lytchett Heath, September 1923. *Courtesy of Lord Rockley.*

Above: Lytchett Heath, on acid Dorset heathland, grew spectacular quantities of *Erica lusitanica,* which was sold as a cut flower at Covent Garden market. Alicia (standing) helping the dispatch with Walter Barfoot, the under gardener for 46 years. *Courtesy of Lord Rockley.*

Below: Howard Carter (right) is well-known as the discoverer of the tomb of Tutankhamun in November 1922. A Norfolk lad from Swaffham, he had been recruited as a sketch-recorder of archaeological finds by Alicia's father, and her *History...* contains several watercolours of gardens done by him. *Copyright: Griffith Institute, University of Oxford.*

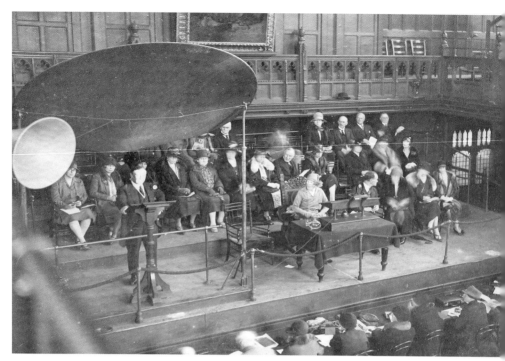

Above: Alicia was involved in the charitable movement to promote emigration to the British colonies throughout her adult life. Here she chairs a meeting of the Society for the Overseas Settlement of British Women at Church House, London, 31st October, 1928.
Courtesy of Lord Rockley.

Below: Alicia and adult daughter Margaret at Mareeba Station, Australia, with members of the Country Women's Association.
Courtesy of Lord Rockley.

Left: Alicia holds bouquets of New Zealand wild-flowers presented to her and to Margaret by the Victoria League in Auckland in September 1926. These flowers - and the need for a handy guide to identify them - inspired her book *Wild Flowers of the Great Dominions of the British Empire* which came to fruition in 1935. *Courtesy of Lord Rockley.*

Below: Alicia and her husband Evelyn leave Victoria Station by the Orient Express, 5th January 1933 on their way to Cairo for the International Railway Congress. Evelyn's wealth was built in part on railway investments and most of Alicia's botanical travels were by train. *Courtesy of Lord Rockley.*

Above: Evelyn (as Lord Rockley), centre, with members of the Royal Commission on Safety in Mines at Bestwood Pit, 12th March 1936. Mining and railways were strong interests of the family.
Courtesy of Lord Rockley.

Below: Evelyn and Alicia on the terrace of Lytchett Heath on 12th May 1939, when they opened the garden for the Queen's nurses.
Courtesy of Lord Rockley.

I owe an immense debt of gratitude for their extreme kindness to me during my early career. It was the Amherst Egyptian collection, perhaps the largest and most interesting collection of its kind then in England, that aroused my longing for that country. It gave me an earnest desire to see Egypt.'[9]

In the winter of 1894–5 the Amhersts travelled to Egypt where they had many interactions with the Newberry family, Howard Carter and the Petries. It is hard to understand now what a part of the 'social season' of the aristocracy a winter visit to Egypt was. An influential family like the Amhersts would be sure to meet others they knew and entertain, or be entertained by, them either on board boats or in hotels such as the famous Winter Palace at Luxor. Thomas Cook was one firm that hired boats – *dahabiyeahs* – on the Nile which acted as floating hotels. Alicia's journal from part of this trip remains[10] and makes clear how important comfort was. She called the journal *Didlington up the Nile*. 'This was said by my great uncle Charles Fountaine when my father in 1860 asked him if he would go up the Nile with him – no easy matter in those days. His reply was "yes, if it is Didlington up the Nile!" He had no wish to rough it; he was a fine photographer and his wife Aunt Rose a help to mother.'

The trip was important to Alicia because it showed where many of the Amherst treasures had been collected and affirmed her friendship with the Newberrys and Carter. It also showed the connection between her interest in archaeology and garden history that was a feature of her friendship with Percy Newberry (it was on board the dahabiyeah *Hathor* that she received the first proof of the illustration list for her *History*).

So the Amhersts, with daughters Sib, Flo, Maggie and Alicia, set off from Victoria on 4th December 1894 by train and boat via Dover-Calais to Paris, where they enjoyed the opera and ballet. On the 5th they proceeded to Marseille by train and, on the next day, to San Raphael where they remarked on the immense growth of Cannes and 'houses all along to Antibes and down the Cap'. On the 8th at Bordighiera, Alicia recalled: 'The sketching mania very strong, the garden of palms and roses looking tropical and soft grey olives as a backdrop. We had to sketch. Sat in the garden most of the morning … it is hotter today … mother rather tired.' On to Genoa they went and then Rome where, like all tourists, they pretended to drink at the Trevi Fountain. On Thursday

14th they had a carriage ride: 'The morning was lovely and the Campania on one side and Rome in the distance and soft pines and full cypresses were all so pretty and the peasants coming in and the fresh morning added to the picture.' The view from the Capitol she pronounced 'All quite beautiful'. Then on to Naples with a journey she labelled as 'very brigandy and the people look wild still' and thence to Pompeii with Vesuvius, 'the cruel mountain looking as if it could do the same thing again whenever it liked.' On Saturday 16th they went to Brindisi and thence on the SS *Arcadia* for Port Said. This journey took them past Cephalonia and Crete where they were allowed to see the 700 hp engines and stoke a furnace themselves. On the 19th they approached a 'cold and wet' Port Said and went through the Suez Canal to Ismailia and so to Cairo for Alicia's first impressions of desert: 'We got our first sight of real desert, miles of sand stretching right all over. Some of the Arabian hills showed up in the distance and lots of camels here and there and the sand so soft and inviting with ripples marked like the seashore and in places patches of pebbles which shone in the sun like water.'

The scenes gave Alicia a love of the desert which she never lost. The first town they came to was, importantly, 'where the paschts at home came from'; they then saw the pyramids which 'stood out large and mysterious in the far distance'.

While staying at the Hotel Continental in Cairo they visited the Gizeh Museum with the Newberrys and entertained them to dinner on Christmas Day. They also visited a mosque to see the dancing dervishes – 'Some seem to get giddy and others not a bit but it made one giddy to watch. They were more graceful than I thought they would be.' On Saturday 29th they visited the pyramids of Giza and rode to the Sphinx on camels before boarding for a trip to Sakhara, where they were joined by the Newberrys, to visit the tomb of Tye with the 'roof of the chamber all blue stars'.

The 8th of January was Lady Amherst's birthday. They went to Beni Hasan and on donkeys to the tombs which Newberry had traced. On the 10th, a particularly hot day, they 'found the place where Howard Carter found our statues just outside the sun temple'. On the 11th they visited the tomb of Khenaten, Amenhotep IV of the 18th dynasty.

It was very hot, full of bats and smelt of them and we were told not to hold the walls going down the steep steps because of the snakes. The subjects carved in relief had once been painted and were fine and unlike any others except those of the tombs in the snake pit … the suns rays [*sic*] some of them really very well drawn, spirited and not so conventional. Below another flight of steps was the mummy pit 30 feet deep, now filled up as it was so dangerous.

By the 19th they had continued by *dahabiyeah* to within sight of Karnak where they met up with the Petries. Alicia commented on Karnak: 'It seemed very like a dream seeing things one had known all one's life.' They anchored at Luxor on the 20th, after lunch:

> … the Egertons of Tatton came on board. Howard Carter was working with Mr Naville cleaning out the temple of Der-el-bareh. He is particularly impressed with the temple of Amenhotep III, Seti I and Ramses II. I think it is the most impressive building I have ever seen, the golden light at sunset on the massive pillars and in the distance a perfect sunset sky and Nile, the hills of Thebes beyond is quite a never to be forgotten scene.

On 21st January she noted that work had intervened: 'I got the proofs for my book illustration by the mail on Sunday evening so had to spend some time arranging them. It is blowing quite hard and there are quite waves.'

On the 24th they reached Aswan and 'the Sheik's Hill with tombs excavated by Sir Francis Grenfell, from one of which our mummy case of Ampetti came …' She then went down with a fever and on 26th January 'spends all day marking proofs for illustrations'.

On the 29th she was restored and gave a fine instance of the interest in colour which inspired her in her sketching:

> The first morning light is quite perfect. Nothing in this world by the way of chromes and cadmiums could be bright enough for the sand. Even in one's hand it is golden and with the morning sun on it it is brilliant. There is hardly any cultivation beyond a strip of 20 yards and beyond it *golden* sand with bits of boulders on the tops of the undulations and in places steeper rocky hills, pretty shapes and jagged with rocks, the rocks themselves rounded granite looking mostly black but pink in places and the hollows of the hills filled with sand like golden snowdrifts stretching smooth to the water's edge. In some places no cultivation and the sand falls like waterfalls

of red and gold straight to the river. We simply rave about the sand and try in vain to get the colour in our sketches.

On 1st February they visited Abu Simbel and saw crocodiles.

The Amherst's usual routine was to rise at 6.00a.m., breakfast at 7.00a.m., visit in the morning before lunch at noon, and rest from 1.00–3.00p.m. Monday 11th was spent shopping in the bazaars. This was the mid-point in the tour; and they left Aswan to turn north on the 13th regretting only the crush of *dahabiyeahs*. On Sunday 24th Howard Carter came to dine with Mr Naville. It was the first of several days he spent with them, sleeping on board. On the 25th they went to the Valley of the Kings.

> We looked at H. Carter's drawings after lunch and then saw the temples. The mummys they had found about a fortnight ago were in the house [(M. Navilles)]. They were most lucky in finding the tomb untouched. Three mummy cases in all, all perfect with … two Anubises sitting on the coffins and four Horuses … we saw where it was found but the mummy pit was filled in … H. Carter came back to dine and sleep on board.

On Shrove Tuesday (the 26th) she writes: 'The Newberrys dined with us and Howard Carter came to dine and sleep as he did every night when we were there.'

The diary ends on Thursday 28th with quite a picture of the social life of the time: 'The Comptons dined and Dr May and the Newberrys and Crosleys [*sic*] came in the evening, we had quite a party, the boat all lit up with little lights and very prettily decorated with palms. They brought a bundle of 100 branches on board which made it nice and cool looking and green. Lord Compton sang to us most beautifully.'

Unfortunately, the two final volumes of Alicia's diary are missing but enough is there to show her close connection with the Newberrys and with Carter, and how they ran parallel to her work on the *History*. There is nothing to suggest that Alicia's relationship with Percy Newberry was anything more than one based on their mutual interests in archaeology and garden history. Indeed, after returning from Egypt she wrote to him: 'The first "lotus" of the season was bought me from the hot house [at Didlington] this morning, we feel that it has flowered to bring good luck to you, so send it with all our best congratulations.' Percy Newberry had become engaged.[11]

4

A History of Gardening in England, 1891–7

The *History* had its genesis in a suggestion by Percy Newberry in 1891. In 1889 he had written some articles on the history of English gardening to the middle of the sixteenth century in the *Gardener's Chronicle,* modestly under the initials P.E.N., and suggested that Alicia might like to take them on further. Her aim was to cite gardens 'as illustrations of each successive fashion' so as to 'serve as a handbook by which to classify gardens, and fix the dates to which they belong'. Her archive in the Chelsea Physic Garden clearly shows this was at first intended to be a collaborative project with joint attribution. There is a proof jacket dated 'London 1892' with the names of The Hon. A. Amherst and P.E. Newberry on the spine. But by 1894 it was clear that Newberry was finding archaeology more pressing. She wrote to him on 12th January 1894 (while on her Egyptian tour): 'I still hope that in spite of all your other work you will find time to write an introductory chapter. I shall leave the ancient Britons and Romans entirely to you.'[1] But it was never to be and the publication finally came out in her own name. Percy and Alicia's intellectual paths had divided – his into archaeology and hers into garden history.

   The importance of Alicia's book was that it started so early in British history, and this was partly because of the author's familiarity with her father's antiquarian interests. She had discovered, in the library of Trinity College, Cambridge, a very early manuscript called *The Feate of Gardening* by 'Jon the Gardener', which she believed to be fourteenth century. She wished her translation and annotation of it to be presented to the Society of Antiquaries, of which her father was a member. On 2nd December 1893 she wrote to Newberry that she feared it 'is not so old as we thought at first' and that the Society of Antiquaries would not be interested in it if it was fifteenth century. She thought it dated from 1440 and was 'the earliest original treatise on Gardening'.

Alicia's work on *The Feate* was done in association with Professor Walter Skeat, whom she persuaded to become interested despite his other work, in mid-December 1892. When it was published, in *Archaeologia*, Vol. liv (1894), she made clear she considered it the 'first practical treatise on gardening' and that it was its practicality which made it valuable: 'John Gardener must certainly have been a practical gardener, as the poem is a series of most sensible and reasonable instructions for growing fruits, herbs, and flowers, and his work is singularly free from the superstitious beliefs in astrology, and the extravagant fancies and experiments in grafting and rearing plants, especially fruit trees, so prevalent in the writing of the period.'

The Feate eventually became absorbed in the *History* but it was important that she had identified something so early. On 7th December 1894 she wrote to Newberry that most of the work had been confirmed as 1440–50 but that the last third of the work was mid-sixteenth century. However, she would 'still like it published – It is still about the earliest thing is it not?'

Her paper was read to the Society of Antiquaries by her father (it would have been considered improper for her to have read it herself) on 9th March 1895. It was 'well received by the Antiquaries present' and subsequently printed. It was her first publication. Meanwhile, she was pressing ahead with the *History* itself, including detailed study of the monastic accounts known as the Norwich rolls with help from Mr Kirk, 'an expert researcher to help me to read them'. On 2nd April 1894 she wrote: 'I never thought I should work so hard at it when I began. I did not realise all I undertook.' By 15th March 1895: 'I find the book grows and grows! I have read and hunted up a lot, & am making enquiries about old gardens – I have had a paper of questions printed … & hope to get information that way. The more I go on the more I get interested in the work.' Copies of her 'proforma' questionnaire remain in the archive of the Chelsea Physic Garden and show that she was asking for information on date of construction and design, details of 31 different features ranging from mounts to vineries, 'Any special plants grown or any peculiar way of growing them', historical events connected to the garden, and the existence of archives, published accounts, engravings or photographs.

One of the characteristics of Alicia's work was her meticulous attention to detail. For example, she produced a glossary for *The Feate* and on 15th January 1895 she told Newberry: 'There are 98 flowers mentioned and many require a good deal of research to identify. It all helps with the book as I am learning all the time and keep coming across things that help but it impedes the actual writing down of the history. The more I write the more I find I have a lot to learn and find out before the book is in any way complete.'

After Alicia returned from Egypt she continued to work on her bibliography (which proved to be one of the *History*'s finest features). She reported it to Newberry as nearly complete 'down to the year 1837' on 18th October 1895 and that the book should be out in November. 'It is so very different from the little book we originally talked over. Instead of a small 8vo with about 8 chapters and as many illustrations, it is large 8vo with 13 chapters, 65 illustrations and 400! pages … although I am very glad to have finished, it has been a great pleasure and interest.'

A History of Gardening in England was published by the antiquarian book dealer and publisher Bernard Quaritch in 1895, initially to subscribers at 15s and later at 21s. The reviews were very positive and picked up its important features. First, its completeness ('This beautiful and interesting volume … is really the most complete history of English gardening we possess'[2]), second, its extensive bibliography ('… to complete this learned treatise there is a bibliography of works on English gardening … Its Index, too, is most carefully worked out, and to those who desire knowledge … and have a fair-sized hole in their library shelf, the book will be valuable'[3]) and, third, its readability ('She has produced a work which is thorough enough to satisfy the scholar, while at the same time it is so lightly handled that it does not repel the general reader'[4]). *The Times* of 6th December 1895 commented: '… she treats gardens not merely from a horticultural or technical point of view, but in all their variety of historical, literary and personal associations.' *The Gardeners' Chronicle* of 21st December 1895 showed that her first foray into print had prepared the audience for the *History*: 'Miss Amherst is well known to all lovers of old gardening literature for her publication in last year's *Archeologia* of the "Fifteenth Century Treatise on Gardening by Mayster Jon Gardener" and the careful way in which that interesting treatise was edited by her, showed that she was well capable of larger efforts in the literature of gardening.'

Alicia's *History* laid the foundation for the later study of garden history and defined the parameters for its scholarly methods. She worked from original sources meticulously footnoted, she produced a detailed and comprehensive bibliography and her wide education enabled her to map horticultural history alongside social, political and technological developments without special pleading for any particular point of view. That was quite some achievement in an age of the partisan: Reginald Blomfield promoting the formal style and William Robinson the new 'wild gardening'.

The *History* was also reviewed in the *Quarterly Review* of July 1896 by, Alicia believed, Gertrude Jekyll.[5] This was before Gertrude had written the books which made her name (published between 1899 and 1925) and when she was primarily a horticultural journalist. She sounded a critical note but then became more accommodating:

> The work which we have placed at the head of this article purports to be a history of gardening in England. The subject is a vast one – too vast indeed to be adequately treated in a single volume of any ordinary proportions. Nevertheless, a careful division of the subject into historical periods and a praiseworthy abstention from discursiveness have enabled Miss Amherst to produce a clear and very readable sketch of the history of gardening. She has brought to her task a knowledge of practical gardening, a fondness for old garden literature, a very evident love of her subject, and much of the subject, and much of the indispensable faculty for taking pains.

However she recommended that Alicia pay less attention to the early period and more to the nineteenth century which had 'long outshone all that has gone before' in developments of the science of horticulture, botany, hybridisation and the collection of plants. She also wished that Alicia had been able to be more partisan over the loss of so many formal gardens to Capability Brown[6] – implicitly undermining two of Alicia's greatest contributions, the study of medieval history and her objectivity.

There is no indication or record that Alicia ever met Gertrude Jekyll, although they certainly had a common friend in Ellen Willmott. Their outlooks were fundamentally different. Alicia was twenty-two years younger and had a much more positive attitude to the future than did Gertrude who, in the last decade of the nineteenth century was bemoaning the spread of industrialisation, urbanisation and the loss of quality in craft which was common in the Arts and Crafts movement.[7]

Alicia's own memories of the publication of her book were later given to her children:

> My 'History of Gardening in England' came out in the autumn of 1895, and no one could have been more astonished than I was at its huge success. Quaritch, the publisher, made an offer for a 2nd edition, three weeks from the day it first came out. His offer was double to what he had given for the 1st – £50, instead of £25. I was advised to refuse and, within a few days, he offered me £250.[8]

Alicia was very robust about the value of her work, at least by the time of the Third Edition in 1910 (published by John Murray). She states in its Preface:

> Although details of countless gardens in the Kingdom have been published, no other attempt has been made to classify or arrange them chronologically. No one else has tried to review consecutively the changes which have taken place, and the fashions which have prevailed, or to follow the process of development which has gradually led up to the modern garden, and I believe this volume still remains the only work of reference on the subject.[9]

Quaritch, however, was initially quite a wet blanket. In a letter sent to her at St Raphael on 6th March 1897[10] he stated prosaically: 'The first edition sold so quickly because it was a novelty – and came in nicely as a Christmas gift.' He reported that the Second Edition '… sells slowly but steadily. It will take however many years before the present large edition of 1500 copies is exhausted.' On 26th May he then sent her £100 as the final instalment owing.

The Chelsea Physic Garden's archive contains an annotated proof set of the *History* worked upon in September to November 1894 and August 1895. It shows from the illustration list that paintings of the Mount, Rockingham, the Garden House, Loseley and Littlecote were all by Howard Carter – and, indeed, his signature appears clearly in the bottom right hand corner of these. Paintings of Bramham and Hall

Barn were by Vernet, his elder brother. It was this list she was working on in Egypt while on the dahabiyeah *Hathor* on 21st January 1895 while the wind blew hard.

Alicia's knowledge of Latin helped her with her studies of the accounts of the monastery gardens of Westminster Abbey, St Swithin's Priory, Winchester, Abingdon Abbey, Ely Place in London, and Norwich. In the case of the Gardeners' Rolls of the Priory, Norwich, from 1340 to 1529, she had worked on them with R.E.G. Kirk, deducing horticultural practice from the financial accounts. She had worked hard on the Sloane manuscripts in the British Museum as well as the herbals which she had access to at Didlington, including those of Macer and Grosseteste. In everything she tried to ascertain the actual *practice* of horticulture in all its branches, whether it was 'florists feasts', rush-strewing, the attempts to introduce mulberry cultivation, moles as garden pests, town gardening, the history of plant classification or the operation of the 'still room'. Other sources investigated included the State Papers of the Cecils (Sir William and his son Thomas) from 1521–87, James I's Patent Roll giving Grant to the Master, Wardens and Assistants of the Gardeners of London, and the Index to the six folio volumes of Parliamentary Rolls from Henry III to Henry VII. These gave access to the practices of the Keepers of the Garden in the Tower (Robert Jayne), the King's and Queen's Garden in the Tower (Richard Barry), the Garden at Eltham Palace (Robert Palmer) and at Greenwich (George Kene). Ministers' accounts for the Diocese of Hereford and the Duchy of Lancaster were also explored. She was always respectful of practical horticulturists, such as innovative fruit growers, nurserymen and market gardeners, while at the same time being able to detail developments in landscape and garden design. That would be far less possible nowadays when the professions have almost totally split.

The publication of the *History* brought her instant recognition. In 1896 she was given the Freedom of the Worshipful Company of Gardeners, 'an honour which for some years I was the only lady to possess and of which I am extremely proud'.[11] Soon after, she received the Freedom of the City of London itself. The *History* also brought her influential friends, like Ellen Willmott who wrote on 17th May (probably 1896, but she rarely dated letters) from her villa 'Tresserve' in the South of France, addressing her as 'My dear Miss Amherst'. She had visited the Amhersts that afternoon and continued: 'I was shy about writing to congratulate you upon the great success of your book but I will not let the same reason prevent me from letting you [know] how happy I have been to know you at last …' By 1902 the friendship had progressed enough to deserve the greeting 'Dearest Allie', and the signature, 'Your affectionate friend'.[12] It remains a mystery, however, why Alicia never got more involved with the Royal Horticultural Society – as Ellen Willmott did – nor was recognised by it or served on its committees. Alicia's attentions later became more political and it is probable that politics took up more and more time.

The *History* had the effect of bringing Alicia into demand as a speaker and an advisor on matters horticultural. On 12th February 1897, Mr Northover, the sub-editor of the *Journal of the Royal Institution of British Architects*, wrote to invite her remarks on a paper by one of its new Honorary Associates, H.E. Milner, entitled 'The Garden in Relation to the House'. Milner, who had published *Art and Practice of Landscape Gardening* in 1890, gave an eloquent exposition of its theory:

I maintain that we should carry out in the parts surrounding the house the architectural feeling of the design in the terraces, walls, steps, basins, beds and so form a base; that we can still have the dignified and quiet delight of formal work – not a narrow curtailment of the whole design. But I insist that there is in addition a broader treatment beyond – a work difficult to proportion in relation to foreground, to broad lawn-spaces, to grouping and choosing trees and shrubs for effect in size and colour, to directing the eye to desired points, to taking advantage of climate and character of the place either natural or acquired, to provision of light and shade in the undulation of the ground, and to a knowledge of horticulture. This art – gardening is, I venture to assert, far beyond the limitations of formal work only, for it can apply to balance and proportion of the latter, and in addition, present to us a noble conception of art-work – its execution of outline, surface-formation, and grouping and draw into the picture the greater, broader, varied landscape.

In reply Alicia took a much more horticultural line. She agreed that the garden design should accord with the period but opined:

… surely the first object of a garden is to make a suitable place for growing plants, and never were there so many new 'outlandish' flowers in this country as there are today, and they ought to be taken into consideration when new designs for gardens are being made. Just as the Elizabethan house had now to be modified to suit modern requirements so the garden even when laid out on old formal lines should be made more suitable to the numerous modern additions to the garden. The material we have to work with now is finer than it ever was, and yet to arrange these treasures of nature in a way to form a suitable surrounding to a house, is no easy task. These remarks suggest themselves to me from having noticed some gardens of good design spoilt by the want of suitable plants and still more, most beautiful groups of plants, trees and flowers, losing much of their charm from lack of proper design. To grow certain plants in the North of England a walled garden, or one sheltered by hedges might be imperative. Again in the South or West so many sub-tropical plants may be naturalised it would not be in the interests of Horticulture to limit the garden by restricting the design.[13]

This debate – whether a garden is primarily a design or primarily a place for plants – still rages today. It is clear which side Alicia was on. The background to it then, of course, was the phenomenal rate of new plant introductions in Victorian times, particularly from the Himalayas, the Americas and China.

Alicia was now accepted as an authority on gardens[14] and this propelled her into a rôle in saving the Chelsea Physic Garden. In 1941 she wrote to her children, recalling how it happened:

I felt I ought to know more botany and, as I had come to know the Physic Garden while writing my book, I attended lectures of Mr G.J. Baker of Kew.[15] I think it must have been his suggestion and that of Sir William Thisleton Dyer [sic], which made Sir Henry Longley, head of the Charity Commission, summon me to make me give evidence. The garden had belonged to the Apothecaries' Company; they said they could not afford to carry it on. The Cadogan estate said if it was no longer any use, as a garden, they would build on it. I was terrified in giving evidence, although they hid the shorthand typist behind a screen. I know I helped to save it, as I said the poor garden had been starved and all it wanted was several good cartloads of manure to make it capable of supplying all the Polytechnic schools of London with specimens for their lectures. The trustees of the London Parochial [who took over the running of the garden from the Apothecaries], appointed me one of the first Board of Management, I think in 1900. I have been re-appointed every 3 years since and I have only just resigned – 1941. It has been a great interest and joy all my life.[16]

5

The Women's Issue: Horticultural Colleges for Ladies, and Women's Suffrage, 1895–1910

In the closing decades of the nineteenth century it was widely perceived that Britain had a population imbalance – too many women, and too many by about a million unmarried females. This was partly a result of the population explosion in the first half of the nineteenth century and, perversely, the government policy of encouraging emigration. Whole families had emigrated but more men than women in total had gone to jobs in the colonies. So there was pressure to enable women to emigrate safely and end the imbalance at home. In 1889 several charitable groups which had been operating since 1884 came together to found the British Women's Emigration Association.[1] There was also pressure to open up more employment opportunities for women, and one of these was in horticulture.

The Women's Branch of the Swanley Horticultural College in Kent was formed in June 1891 in order to make available 'the Art and Science of Horticulture, the advantages of which, up till that date, had been reserved for men only'. In 1896 its Annual Report made clear that this initiative was concerned with women's livelihoods both in Britain and the colonies – '… for those intending to practise gardening, whether as managing their own estates, as intending colonists, as market gardeners, as accepting appointments as head-gardeners on private property, or under market-gardeners or specialists, or as lecturers and practical teachers of horticulture'. Colleges soon began to spring up like mush-rooms and in 1903 Swanley, with 63 students, reserved itself for women only.

In 1899 Alicia sent a paper to the International Congress on 'Market Gardening for Women'. Perhaps it was this that prompted Lady

Warwick to write to her about her new school at Reading, the Lady Warwick Hostel, which had 21 students and was apparently self-sufficient after only four months: 'I am most anxious to get you on my <u>Executive Committee</u>, knowing how keen an interest you take in horticulture, and feeling how invaluable your help and advice will be to us … <u>Please</u> do not refuse! as I want your name <u>so much</u> for our Horticultural side.' Alicia agreed to become a patron and enclosed her annual subscription, but this was not enough for Lady Warwick who, in a telegram of 18th February 1899, badgered her into agreeing to join their 'General Committee' which met only once a year. Few people turned down Daisy Warwick, society beauty and favourite mistress of the Prince of Wales, but Alicia was obviously busy.[2]

She became active in trying to find places for female graduates from horticultural colleges. Letters remain from a Mr Walker who wrote to her on 10th December (no year) requesting a recommendation for a place for his 24-year-old daughter, 'a Swanley diplomee and devoted to the work'. Sometimes new schools failed and one Magdalen Mitchell, who had run the School for Horticulture for Ladies at Aberglaslyn in Torquay (which included a 'Special Course for Colonial Training') wrote on 9th June 1900 to ask for a recommendation for a position now she was out of work.[3]

Alicia reported on the progress of the movement for women in horticulture in the Third Edition of her *History* in 1910. She observed that there was good progress, 'in spite of a strong prejudice against women taking up the work seriously', and noted:

> Of those who complete their training, about eighty per cent keep up their gardening and of these about forty become private or jobbing gardeners, about ten take to market gardening, about ten become teachers or lecturers, and about twenty garden in their own houses, or otherwise lead open-air lives. Other teaching centres have since been opened, and the number of women who take up gardening as a profession is on the increase. The movement is not confined to the country, but there are women's horticultural colleges both in Europe and America. The very idea of a lady being employed as a head-gardener, with men and boys working under her, was so astonishing that the suggestion naturally met with much opposition, but the able way in which ladies have discharged the multitudinous duties of such a position is already disarming criticism.[4]

She reported that twelve Swanley students had become head gardeners in 1908 – the same year the Hon. Frances Wolseley had published her book on women in horticulture from her School at Glynde in Kent.

Alicia eventually joined the committee of the Country and Colonial Training College for Ladies at Arlesey in Bedfordshire, which had been founded in 1908 under the Presidency of Lady Frances Balfour. It supplied 'a thorough training in Home Farm Management for ladies intending to emigrate, or for those who, REMAINING AT HOME, wish to manage their own property or small holdings.' The Principal, Miss Turner, advertised that she had 'special facilities for acquiring information as to the different Colonies and there are always good openings in the Dominions over Seas for competent, well-trained women'.[5] Students were entered for the RHS and NDH exams after two years at 80 guineas per annum.

The crucial point about these colleges was not that they were female but that they trained 'ladies'. One of the main recommendations was that 'ladies' (who had been able to command servants) had the appropriate manner and confidence to give instruction to male gardeners under their command. Frances Wolseley was adamant on this point. For opponents of women in horticulture, such as the then Hon. Secretary of the Royal Horticultural Society, the Revd. W. Wilks, the work required strength and, he felt, women could not command men. To an enquiry by Alicia he replied:

I am afraid I cannot help you. I know of no woman gardener who has what you want in all round knowledge so as to (sic) able to direct the different departments. I do not believe such a person exists. Miss Jekyll herself would not be able to take such a post. My real objections to women gardeners are twofold. I have no objection (quite otherwise) to women undertaking work in the world which is (a) suited to them and (b) to which they are suited. Women gardeners are a most decidedly retrograde step. I venture to think that no man can be a good gardener, & be able to direct others unless he has gone through the 'dirty druggery' (sic) of the garden and no woman should ever in my opinion be sent to do that. It is man's work ... Nor do I think that women are physically strong enough for much of the heavy lifting and clay digging which is unavoidable. Thus you see that in my idea (a) the work is not suited to women (b) women are not suited to the work and to put women to it is to go back a big step in the emancipation of your sex.

The underlining is in red, and presumably by Alicia. He ended the letter by commenting: 'That women are admirably fitted for some of the lighter and more delicate operations of higher gardening is an altogether dift (sic) position. Forgive me …'[6]

Alicia must have found the Revd. Mr Wilks' comments enraging. On 14th June 1900 she sat with her parents at the top table, two places away from him, at a dinner organised by the Worshipful Company of Gardeners. One wonders if the subject was discussed. Even worse was a letter of 23rd June 1905 from Ernest Ebblewhite of the same Worshipful Company informing her that, despite her having the Freedom of the Company, the Installation Dinner of 5th July was 'for gentlemen only'.

Alicia had strong views on what was appropriate work for women and how it could be achieved. She was not supportive of Thiselton-Dyer's attempt to get women students from Swanley into knicker-bockers at Kew so that they looked as much like men as possible and so would not distract them. Of the 39 students from Swanley in its first year of admitting women she comments:

> Many of these never intend to be anything but amateurs, but several have already passed out of the College to take head gardener's places. Students from Swanley have also been allowed to continue their education at Kew, but the somewhat arbitrary restrictions which oblige women to wear so-called 'rational' knickerbocker dress has deterred many from making use of this advantage. The herbaceous borders at Kew, however, were last year tended entirely by women, and Mr Thiselton-Dyer was satisfied that they had never been better cared for. Although some of the work of a gardener is hard, it is an art in which neatness and dexterity play so important a part that it is a calling eminently suited to women.

She was interested in what women could achieve and also in the opening up of horticulture to women as a profession instead of a pastime. 'This is undoubtedly an inestimable benefit to women. There has been in the past so much overcrowding, and consequent low standard of remuneration, in the teaching profession and among secretaries, clerks and typists that the fresh air and wholesome life of the garden has indeed been a welcome outlet for many a girl.' Clearly, the point was improvement in employment options for women. Ever practical, she counselled that it was wrong to cut training short as it would 'damage the prospects in that field of employment for all women that come after them', and she therefore stressed the importance of 'a horticultural certificate which is a reliable guarantee of efficiency.'[8]

It should not be supposed that because Alicia was so keen on helping women into horticulture she was a supporter of women's suffrage. The opposite was true and for interesting reasons. Alicia was horrified at the violent excesses of the suffragettes who, by 1910, were burning churches. Around that time she was encouraged to write for the National League for Opposing Woman Suffrage and in their journal No. 38 she contributed an article entitled 'Substance and Shadow'. It was an intelligently argued piece in which she sought to show that:

> ... women have much real power in their hands as it is, and that by grasping at the Parliamentary franchise they would find that in reaching out towards a shadow they had lost the substance ... Greatly as law-abiding citizens despise suffragists' violent methods, they cannot but admire their energy. But it seems to the anti-suffragist that even half that amount of energy spent in doing work to which they now have access would produce far more salutary and substantial results.

Her argument was that there was lots of useful political work women might do in the municipal field including tasks 'which cannot be so well performed by men Councillors'. Women's suffrage was achieved by many small steps and one of them was, indeed, the Qualification of Women (County and Borough Councils) Act of 1907. She noted that under the Public Health, Housing and Local Government Acts they could be concerned with 'sanitary conditions and overcrowding generally, with asylums, fever hospitals, infection and isolation, inspection of noxious trades, laundries, home-workers' dwellings, common lodging-houses, baths, washhouses, dispensaries, etc.' Further opportunities were open under the Children's Act 1908, the Midwives Act, the 1902 Education Act, the Municipal Corporations Act and the Old Age Pensions and Unemployed Workmen's Acts. She was really arguing for a division of labour with women contributing primarily in the sphere of social welfare, 'without encroaching on paving, lighting, water, tramway, buildings, finance, and other matters where the experience of men should prevail'. She was convinced that women were too apathetic in taking up this work. She saw this as a 'dereliction of duty' and was particularly keen that moderate women came forward:

In dealing with all these subjects, it is the very virtues despised by the suffragists that are most needed. If women are to carry weight in a council of men, there must be calm and tactful reasoning, without violent self-assertion, and they must show themselves capable of firm but sympathetic management, devoid of ostentatious aggressiveness. If educated women with leisure are sincere in their desire to help to lift something of the weight which crushes women toilers, they must get into close touch with them and their surroundings, and there could be no better opportunity than by serving on public bodies.

She was, however, very forward-looking in some of her recommendations, including that of a quota being reserved for women (still a contentious strategy today) – 'The ultimate aim should be that of establishing a recognised custom, that a due proportion (say about 10 per cent) of all seats on Municipal Councils should rightly be filled by women; and legislation might eventually secure a certain number of places for them among the Aldermen.' This was in line with a Royal Commission Report on the Poor Law which had recommended that the Public Assistance Committee should comprise one-third women and the committee on maternity be entirely female.

That work was needed to improve slum conditions had been made clear by the Committee on Physical Deterioration. Women, said Alicia, were best placed 'to dispel ignorance, and bring brightness … in an official capacity, armed with all the authority of the local governing body …' She believed that the 'opinion of women taking a quiet but active part in the forefront of women's legitimate work, would command much more respect than the noisy parade and demonstration of the Suffragist' and that in 'Local Government work, the very fact that women do not have a Parliamentary vote is a source of strength. They stand apart from the turbid turmoil of party politics, and can work on municipal councils in the interests of the poorer classes and the prevention of misery, untrammelled by party prejudices.' She ended with a plea for more women to take up municipal work and 'prove the true worth of women, who, instead of clamouring for imaginary "rights", will appreciate their substantial privileges, and accept their real responsibilities.'

Later in her life (about 1941) Alicia looked back on this period, after women had achieved the vote, and makes clear she felt that in 1909 not enough women really knew about politics and were unlikely to use the vote well in parliament.

> I was always opposed to women having the parliamentary vote and so was [my husband] Evelyn. I felt among other reasons there was no legal argument against their being in parliament once they had it, and I felt strongly that they ought if they got it really to use it properly and learn about politics, and I knew very few women before the war were really qualified to use it properly, only a small minority.
>
> I was always strongly in favour of women doing more municipal work, on boards of gardens, schools, borough councils, etc. Mrs Humphrey Woods asked me more than once to write things on this subject and one small pamphlet I wrote about 1909 was ... circulated. I think it was called 'Substance and Shadow'. It was written when suffragettes were screaming for the vote, burning churches and at their worst, and I pointed out how much really useful work they might have been doing instead, in housing, child welfare, etc.[9]

Alicia reveals that her concern was what women could 'do', not their rights. Appropriately to her class, the point was duty and service, and, in the case of the horticultural profession, how women could support themselves in independent lives, whether in Britain or the colonies. At the time, however, it was an issue which divided the family. In 1910 William Amherst (her nephew 'Billy') married Gladys Baggallay, an active suffragette.

6

Marriage, Children and More Writing, 1898–1907

Alicia did not marry until she was 33, quite an age for the time. She was, of course, one of seven sisters and had had to wait until she was 20 to be presented at Court as a débutante. Alicia was tall at five foot eight and had startling blue eyes but she had a strong rather than conventionally beautiful face, unlike her older sister Maggie. She also had a formidable intellect which, at a time when women's colleges were under a quarter of a century old (Girton College, Cambridge was founded in 1869, Newnham in 1871 and Lady Margaret Hall, Oxford in 1878) would tend to get her labelled as a blue stocking. This, of course, did not deter all suitors, but the problem was in finding the right one. According to Oriel Robinson, Alicia's grand-daughter, this meant someone with wealth, preferably with a title and (because of the family's strong Dutch Protestant heritage) not a Roman Catholic. Not that there had been no suitors. Her diary of their Egyptian trip of 1894–5, written in 1908 and kept by her grandson, Lord James Rockley, in the Lytchett Heath library, notes:

> Around 1880 to 1890 I used to go to a small class with mother … with Dr Budge the British Museum instructor … (on hieroglyphics). Unfortunately it had to come to an end as it spoilt it all when (the young professor) fell in love with me and telling mother so when he came to Didlington to study some of the papyruses! We were so annoyed as I could not go on with the lessons! However, we had learnt enough to be of use and when we were in Egypt 1894–5, we could read the names on tombs.

Alicia probably met her future husband, Evelyn Cecil, through her father's political connections, or perhaps via her eldest sister, who had married into the Exeter branch of the Cecils and became Lady William Cecil at St Thomas' Church, Portman Square in 1885. Evelyn was the eldest son of Lord Eustace Cecil, 4th son of the 2nd Marquess of Salisbury of Hatfield House.

As an MP and as nephew and Assistant Private Secretary to the Prime Minister, Lord Salisbury (1891–2 and 1895–1902), he was at the heart of the political life of the country. They married on 16th February 1898 at St George's Hanover Square; it was a glittering occasion, attended by the Prime Minister. The couple were married by the Lord Bishop of Rochester, Alicia's cousin, and she wore rich white satin, given to her by her mother, with a coronal wreath of orange blossom fastened by a large diamond-and-pearl star – the gift of the bridegroom. Lord Amherst gave her a diamond necklace and large heart case, also in diamonds. Very appropriately, her bouquet was provided by the Worshipful Company of Gardeners. It was composed of white roses, orchids, pancratiums, orange blossom and lilac, tied with white satin ribbon and bearing an inscription embossed in silver. Her train was borne by Master Jack, son of Alicia's eldest sister (who was later to increase the family's aristocratic connections by marrying Cornelia Vanderbilt). Three other Cecils were bridesmaids: Blanche, Lady Louisa and the Honourable Beatrice Cecil. Sybil, Margaret and Florence, Gwendolyn Villiers and Miss Jean Drummond made up the remainder, all carrying bouquets of pale pink tulips, lilies of the valley and trails of smilax. What a fragrant affair it must have been![1]

The married couple were received at 8, Grosvenor Square where the display of wedding presents illustrated their royal links (pieces of jewellery were gifts from their Royal and Imperial Highnesses, the Duke and Duchess of Saxe-Coburg). The Master of the Gardeners' Company, N.S. Sherwood, had given them an inscribed silver bowl. Alicia and Evelyn then left for Englemere Hall to stay with her sister and her husband, Lord and Lady William Cecil.

Alicia's marriage brought together her two greatest interests, politics and horticulture. During her honeymoon she developed an article for *The Quarterly* magazine entitled 'Gardening during the Victorian Era'. No doubt reflecting her mood at the time, it is relentlessly upbeat in its celebration of horticultural developments, especially plant breeding, plant nomenclature, new plant introductions, the growth of Kew and its visitor numbers and the popularity of orchids: 'horticulture … [has] advanced one may say by leaps and bounds during this period'. The new couple were enthusiastic supporters of the Empire then at its height – in 1897 Britain ruled one fifth of the land surface of the world and one quarter of its population. Alicia ended her article with a flourish:

> The Floral History of the reign of Queen Victoria opened with the discovery of the Giant Waterlily of the Amazon, rightly named *Victoria regia*, and the promise of this brilliant beginning has been amply fulfilled. Plants have been brought to this country from every garden of those vast dominions on which the sun never sets, and great botanists and Horticulturalists have skilfully tended every new treasure. The peaceful reign of our good Queen has been as propitious in gardening as for all other arts and sciences and like every branch of industry it has received help directly and indirectly from her guiding hand.[2]

The couple spent their London life at 10, Eaton Place, but with country visits to Didlington and Evelyn's father's home, Lytchett Heath, near Poole in Dorset.

> The shooting parties at Didlington continued the first eight years of our married life. One met so many pleasant, cheerful friends, Evelyn enjoyed the sport. I was strong and able to walk out with the ladies in all weathers, and we both enjoyed the social evenings. I remember helping to amuse the other guests at Buscot. Evelyn and I had two little shooting parties at Lytchett, as papa had the Lytchett Matravers shooting for many years. Life was very bright and happy …[3]

According to James Trimbee (see page 107, note 11), Alicia and her eldest sister received cut flowers from Didlington twice weekly to enhance their married quarters.

In 1899–1900, Alicia and Evelyn made a journey which was to change their lives, politically and botanically. It was to Rhodesia and South Africa (before the Boer War) and was helped by their existing social networks.

> It seems extraordinary now, how little people knew about South Africa and our going there seemed quite an adventure. I knew more than many people, through Charlie Villiers and his campaign with Sir Gerald Portal, and, later, he was involved in the Jamieson Raid and tried at the Old Bailey. Sir John Willoughby and Colonel Frank Rhodes were friends who had stayed at Didlington. Frankie Rhodes was a dear and wrote out to his brother, Cecil Rhodes, about us. Evelyn was then Member for East Herts which included

Bishop's Stortford, where the father of the Rhodes had been Rector. Curiously, Rhodes' grandfather had had transactions with Hackney Estate. All this made Evelyn's and my reception by Cecil Rhodes at Cape Town very different from that of an ordinary traveller. Evelyn wrote his impressions in the book 'On the Eve of the War', but I don't think that either of us thoroughly realised, at the time, what an inspiration Cecil Rhodes was. I think Evelyn's and my whole-hearted work for the British Empire really started then ...[4]

The journey turned the couple into even stauncher imperialists. They collected botanical specimens for Kew and in her *History* she records finding 40 new species which were handed to the nurserymen, Messrs Sander. They included a plant of which she was immensely proud and later was depicted in an oil portrait painted by her daughter Maud. It was a yellow form of the Gloriosa Lily, which was given an Award of Merit by the Royal Horticultural Society on 18th June 1901. Alicia had hoped to have it named after her. Sadly, Kew would not agree, but it did name for her a new species of Blood Lily, *Haemanthus cecilae*.[5] This was the beginning of a long correspondence and friendship with successive Directors of the Royal Botanic Gardens and further submissions of South African (and also Australian) plants to the RHS. On their return to the UK Alicia organised a successful exhibition of her sketches of South Africa at a gallery at 118, New Bond Street. The Gloriosa Lily thrived in Alicia's care and by 31st May 1908 she was writing to Colonel Prain, Director of Kew, that it was:

> flowering profusely and is less straggling in growth than superba. The 3 or 4 roots we brought back have increased to about 30. If by chance you would like to have it drawn would you select a good spray out of those sent? I should like to know what you think of it and whether you have it at Kew. I believe it is found this pretty buff yellow in West Africa too. We collected ours in Dec. 1899 – it always comes quite true to colour, which does not look as if it was just a var. of superba anyhow it shows no sign of reverting to type.[6]

The couple also undertook botanical journeys in Europe, often in alpine areas, a clear continuation of Alicia's interest in botany and ecology. In an article for *The National Review* – 'Alpine Flowers at Home' (June 1908) – she described a trip to the Dolomites which they had made, late in the season, in 1903:

We had been finding nothing but ferns and seeds, for flowers were at an end, except for the splendid clumps of the tall gentian, asclepiadea, of the finest blue I have ever seen it, and the edelweiss which grew like daisies in a lawn, on many of the grazing slopes. A steep climb to an altitude of over 7,000 feet took us one day to a rocky ledge near the top of the Rosetta. Clouds were blowing about below us, and the narrow path but at ten inches wide was covered with drifted snow. As we turned over the crest of the ledge and followed along a wall of rock facing east, we noticed every fissure was packed full of this rare little Campanula morettiana. Its tiny blue bells, of a peculiar shape, and long in proportion to the stem, hung out from every crack and corner, while its roots penetrated deeply into the heart of the rock. Masses of it covered the face of the cliff for many yards, the mauve-blue tone showing up delightfully against the almost orange rocks.

Of a trip to Vaud in Switzerland, between the Lakes of Geneva and Thun, she wrote: 'I recall a walk up there, up a valley by a rushing stream to an upland pasture whence the Gruyère cheeses are brought down on mules. Having reached this point, a garden suddenly came in sight where nothing but tall yellow gentians grew side by side with deep purple monk's hood; no herbaceous border could have been more perfectly grouped.'[7]

Alicia often joined Evelyn on journeys overseas involving his political and investment interests in railways. In 1905 she accompanied him to the International Congress in Washington D.C. where he was 'Delegate of the London and South West Railway' (of which he was a Director between 1902 and 1923). They then travelled into Canada where, she recalls, 'I got my first glimpse of Empire Spring Flowers in Eastern Canada. We stayed with Sir George and Lady Drummond, in Montreal; she became very dear to us as "Aunt Julia". In USA we met Theodore Roosevelt and many leading politicians, such as Taft, who became President afterwards, and our friend, Mr Justice Oliver Wendell Holmes, who remained a lifelong friend.'[8]

The experiences of these travels were, eventually, to feed into her final book, grandly titled *Wild Flowers of the Great Dominions of the British Empire* – but not before she had written two others.

Alicia and Evelyn had three children: Margaret, born 27th November 1898; Robert, 20th February 1901; and Maud, 20th October 1904. Her second book, *Children's Gardens*, was published by Macmillan in 1903 on a ten per cent royalty and dedicated to Margaret and Robert. With chapters on spring, summer, autumn and winter, it was intended as a sketch which would give 'the merest mention in unscientific language of some of the most obvious plants and necessary work in each season of the year'.[9] People who write for children on gardening tend to describe their own childhood experiences of it, as Gertrude Jekyll did when, five years later in 1908, she published her own *Children and Gardens*. In Alicia's book it is possible to learn a lot about her own experience of gardening. For her it dispelled cares and instilled patience. She learnt how to hybridise pansies, inspired by her mother who 'told me of her success as a small child with auriculas'.[10] She 'was very fortunate in having a very small glass frame given me when I was quite a little girl, and it was a great delight to me' – in it she succeeded in raising godetias.[11] She described being taught to bud roses and having a garden with a medlar ('because I liked the fruit'), an almond ('for the sake of its blossom') and a quince ('a fancy of mine, as it is so rare'). Reviews of the book were much charmed by her ability to write interesting anecdotes about (and against) herself:

> When I was a very small child I sowed the name of one of my sisters in mustard and cress as a surprise for her birthday. The seeds were put in about ten days before, and the salad was nice and green by the required day in September when all the birthday party were invited to my garden to see it … but alas! it was discovered that I had misspelt the word and there was my fault only too plainly visible in green lines on the brown earth, which no sponge or indiarubber could efface. There was nothing for it but to eat the offending letter first! Imagine my confusion …[12]

Spelling was never her strong point, despite her academic credentials!

It is interesting to compare Alicia's book with Gertrude Jekyll's, which was written at the request of Edwin Lutyens and is clearly the work of someone as deeply interested in architecture as in horticulture: 'If the parents will give the children that greatest of delights, a real, well-built little house, with a kitchen and a parlour, where they can keep house and cook and receive their friends, the garden would naturally be close to it and form part of its scheme.'[13] Both authors thought gardening taught children to be observant, that an undertaking of botany was important, and gave plans of their own first gardens, though Gertrude's was far more concerned to teach about elevations, sections and plans and what we would now call garden design. Gertrude added a chapter about her love of cats and under 'Various amusements' made a telling comment on sandcastles in sandpits: 'Of course it is good if our father happens to be an architect, and sometimes likes to play too, and shows us how to do building.'[14] As the child, so the woman.

Both Alicia and Gertrude, however, assumed, because of their class, that the families of the children who would be reading the book had gardeners to employ and show them how to take cuttings. Alicia kept no fewer than 47 reviews of her book,[15] many of which comment on its value for the Christmas gift market, though many are also critical of its limitation to children of the wealthy:

> … unless children have altered very much in the last thirty years or so, we are afraid they will not see much connection between the little domain where they try so hard to teach nature how to do her work, and the ambitious kind of garden presented to them by Mrs Cecil. Her large views about children's gardens must be justified by the one she seems to have possessed in her own childhood … We certainly never heard before of a child that had enough of its own to make into an ornamental garden with separate beds edged with box, and divided by gravel paths, nor so much space at its command as to grow fruit trees and strawberry plants in one corner of it.[16]

The *Daily News* of 3rd December 1902 thought '… to a child whose garden ground is limited to a few square feet and pocket money to a few round pennies the schemes and ideas of Mrs Cecil's book would only be tantalising.' Not all the press were so class critical, however. *The Standard* of 19th November 1902 stated: 'If this book helps to give impetus to the movement for providing gardens for children in our towns and villages, it will do more for the increase of human happiness than many Acts of Parliament. There is no reason why every public school should not have children's gardens attached to them, even in London.' It is not known how Alicia took the criticism but 1906 saw her at the Country in Town exhibition at Toynbee Hall organised by the Selborne Society: 'For two weeks I went down every day and taught the East-enders how to plant their window boxes, what various seeds looked like coming up. Thousands of people came and were so interested in my sort of lectures and demonstrations.'[17]

In 1907 Archibald Constable published her third book, *London Parks and Gardens*. Like her *History* this was designed to bring together the subject 'as a whole' and covered all the royal and municipal parks, commons and open spaces, squares, burial grounds, the Inns of Court gardens and other historical and private gardens. She defined London as all areas within the then London County Council boundary, and for many years this was the only book on the subject. It is still one of the most complete. It brought Alicia's great talents to the subject: a huge and broad knowledge of the history of London (and of history and architecture in general) plus a great appreciation of trees and what we would now call 'social horticulture'. A century later, the book reads as if the author is a trustee of the Commission for Architecture and the Built Environment (CABE), Learning through Landscapes (LTL) or some such body devoted to the health and social benefits of green space in urban environments. This translated, in Victorian terminology, into the moral and physical improvement of the labouring poor, which was the argument used for opening the Royal Botanic Gardens, Kew, to the general public. It is essentially the same now, as then.

Alicia was deeply aware of the history of the royal parks as hunting and social spaces for the Court and the wealthy. Now she felt there was a new need for them: 'The idea of giving parks as recreation grounds for the poor is such a novel one that no writer would think of noticing their absence in an age when bull-baiting and cock fights were their highest form of amusement.'[18] And one that was particularly important for children: 'The more dingy the houses of children are, the more necessary it must be to bring what is simple, pure and elevating to their minds, and modern systems of teaching are realising this. If public parks can be brought to lend their hand in the actual training, as well as being a playground, they will serve a twofold purpose.'[19]

Her knowledge of municipal politics showed in her description of the development of the city parks' movement, starting with Victoria and Battersea Parks, planted in 1845 and 1857 respectively, progressing through charitable initiatives: 'After the Bill re-organising the disposal of the funds of the London Parochial Charities in 1883, a part of their money was allotted to provide open spaces, and they helped to purchase many of the parks – Clissold, Vauxhall, Ravenscourt, Brockwell and so on.' She correctly credited Octavia Hill, founder member of the

National Trust [which grew out of the Open Space Society], with "efforts to secure open spaces" and with founding the Kyrle Society which developed into the Metropolitan Gardens Association' [though Octavia was actually its energetic Treasurer].[20]

This social benefit, she thought, was rooted in the 'actual horticulture that now engrosses people, the practical cultivation of new and rare plants, the raising and hybridising of florists' varieties ... A thirst for new flowers, for strange combinations of flowers, for revivals of long-forgotten plants and curious shrubs [which] has now taken possession of the large circle of people who profess to be gardeners.'[21] She was aware that, historically, working men's groups had loved flowers. Stoke Newington and Stamford Hill, for example, were where chrysanthemums were first cultivated in England and her father, because of his status in Hackney, had become Patron of the National Chrysanthemum Society.[22] 'The popularity of the chrysanthemum in Battersea Park is so great, that on a fine Sunday there is a string of people waiting their turn of walking through, stretching for fifty yards at least from the green-house to the entrance to the frame-ground.'[23]

Better health was the immediate benefit of parks and green spaces to London – which was increasingly polluted by fog and smoke from coal fires and the electricity generating power stations. The parks were 'lungs of the city'.[24] Even private squares were useful since 'even though they are kept outside the railings the rest of the public receive a benefit from these air spaces and oxygen-exhaling trees.'[25] She also, in effect, predicted the Green Belt legislation: 'These greens scattered around London help to connect the larger areas, thus forming links in the chain of open spaces which enriches London. These natural recreation grounds are the admiration of all foreigners, and a priceless boon to the citizens, ensuring the preservation of green grass and green trees to refresh their fog-dimmed eyes, at no great distance from the throng of city life.'[26]

However, she was practical enough to know that the throngs of people she described could have a deleterious effect, especially on grass. She was also aware that large private gardens, like today, were under threat from ever-increasing house-building ('the temptation to cut them up and build small red villas on the sites is very great'[27]). Her instruction to the East Enders on their window boxes had given her an insight into the therapeutic value of horticulture on any scale – 'for the most part the smaller they [gardens] are, and the less there is to write about them of interest to the general reader, the more they are of value to the happy possessors'.[28]

The methods Alicia adopted when writing her book on London gardens can be seen in the Amherst Archive at Chelsea Physic Garden. She made great use of the British Museum, especially for work on the royal parks where she was clearly concerned to add human interest, impressions of the parks and events held in them, names of Keepers and so on. She always recorded bird life. She used both secondary sources (such as Wheatley's *London Parks & Gardens*) and J.C. Loudon's *Landscape Gardening* of 1840, as well as primary ones like the manuscript records on Burghley-on-the-Hill, including Humphrey Repton's Red Books of April 1795 and 1796. She scoured Parliamentary Papers and Select Committee reports and in July 1906 made considerable effort to obtain lists of trees, sizes of flower beds and borders, and planting schemes for both Hyde Park and Kensington Gardens. She wrote extensively to many people and ran drafts of sections of the manuscript past owners or knowledgeable persons, including the Honorary Secretary of the Metropolitan Public Gardens Association and Lord Redesdale, 'as the King wishes his approval of what I said about Buckingham Palace'.[29] Finally, she visited the gardens extensively. Some of her notes show evidence of their having been written in a jolting cab on the way home. She did not, however, illustrate the book herself, although some of her notebooks contain sketches. Coloured illustrations were provided by her friend, Lady Victoria Manners, who produced watercolours to suit. Not until her final work was Alicia confident enough in her own ability as a watercolourist.

7

Empire, Town and Country, 1899–1909

While Evelyn pursued his political work, Alicia was busy with charitable activities which were directly supportive – they sang with one voice. As well as being MP for Aston Manor, Birmingham (1900–18) and then Birmingham Aston (1918–29), Evelyn also had strong foreign policy interests. After the Boer War, Evelyn and Alicia supported Alfred Milner's plan to reinforce the British victory by flooding the colony with English-speaking immigrants. Since 1884 several charities had been formed to promote colonial emigration. The British Women's Emigration Association (BWEA) had been formed in 1889, sending women to Canada, New Zealand or Australia. This body soon turned its attention to South Africa and in 1901 the South African Colonisation Society (SACS) grew out of it. Alicia was rapidly propelled into a leadership role.

> All our Empire interests seemed to grow rapidly. I don't know quite how it came about that, although I was the newest and youngest of the BWEA, I seemed to get my own way and, finally, within a year, was put in the important post of Chairman of the Transvaal and Orange River. When we formed the South African Expansion Committee, which was to work practically independently of the BWEA, Lord Milner paid my committee, his British one, to work directly with Transvaal Emigration Department at this end. I was directly under the Colonial Office with four men appointed by them and four women, chosen by me. I have just been reading all the early correspondence I had had with leading Johannesburg ladies, while they were still refugees at Cape Town. The first lot of people I saw off, were ten women, as domestic servants, having got, with Evelyn's help, free passages for them in a ship going out to bring back troops. This involved endless letters and interviews between the War Office and the Colonial Office and, in the end, it was Lord Roberts, personally, who managed it – who finally broke the Red Tape. I took the girls myself to Southampton and saw them on a ship.

Looking back, it seems rather wonderful how we worked. Cables came direct from Lord Milner to Chamberlain; 'Please inform Mrs Cecil fifty girls required by November' or similar cable to send out a cook to Lord Tullibardine. There were many applications and, in those days, I did all the interviewing myself. I had many voluntary helpers – I can hardly remember them all, but Gertrude Bell was one of the four on my Committee. As the years went on, from 1901–1908, everything was got on to precise business lines. I think the heaviest year was when we sent out 750 women and only 4 and a half percent were in any way failures. While Lord Milner was still in charge, he came home for a short visit and sent for me to the Colonial Office. I was, indeed, delighted with his greeting. He got up from his large table, held out his hand, saying 'In a year of disappointment, you have not disappointed me.' I felt that was encouragement enough.[1]

This shows a remarkably 'hands on' approach which is fully detailed in the archives of the Women's Library of the London Metropolitan Archive. The connection with Gertrude Bell is interesting. Gertrude, who was later to become significant in the internal politics of Iraq, was three years younger than Alicia and had been educated at Lady Margaret Hall, Oxford where she was the first woman to graduate with a First in History. She had already visited Turkey, Syria and Iran, learnt Arabic in Israel and found the desert as alluring as had Alicia in Egypt. They had a lot in common (not least in opposing women's suffrage) and Gertrude was relied upon as a stalwart. In the summer of 1902 Alicia was ill for two and a half months and could not attend to business, so Gertrude was delegated to inspect fifty general servants assembled at the London Hostel on 22nd October prior to their despatch.[2]

However, things did not go well with the press and by the summer of 1903 they were being publicly criticised (in *The People's Journal*) for having made placements which failed, and for charging too much at their hostels prior to embarkation. That August, with Alicia in Scotland for a holiday, Gertrude ('just returned from a round the world trip') interviewed the party to go out in September. Shortly afterwards, they agreed that every shipment would have a travelling matron in charge. However, it seemed they were getting the reputation of being 'a registry for domestic servants only – this is not what we want', Alicia stated. She was insistent that they place women of a higher class, and/or place them in their own business or on farms: 'Miss Gertrude Bell (one of our committee) who is a most capable worker with very good judgement, is undertaking all the interviewing and selecting of the 6 superior untrained girls and she will very likely write some notes about them.'[3]

Evelyn was Treasurer of SACS from 1901 until 1906 and Alicia was very successful in raising cheques from wealthy donors to support their work. She chaired the Transvaal Committee until 1909 (when she was succeeded by Gertrude Bell) and was active on the Committee of one of the despatching hostels in Paddington. Naturally, much of her interest was in supporting graduates of the Colonial horticultural course at Swanley and in 1905 SACS reported that four Swanley diplomees had been sent out, one to take charge of a 32-acre estate in Natal, one to take up an apprenticeship in a lady's market garden, and two to start a boarding house, poultry farm and market garden on 12 acres in the Transvaal.[4] Alicia joined the SACS Agricultural Committee in 1906.

It is hard to imagine now the pressure that these voluntary committees were under. For example, they had 1,300 applications to emigrate in October 1902. The logistics were difficult and discussions were even held, controversially, to take over the 'concentration camp' huts used in the Boer War to house the immigrants – but they proved too expensive.[5]

Alicia's work with emigration was to continue unchecked, except by illness, until 1938, whereas Gertrude Bell became more and more involved with politics in Iraq.[6] One suspects their paths might have crossed again because they had an acquaintance in common. Gertrude became an ally of Colonel T.E. Lawrence ('Lawrence of Arabia') who was also known to Alicia's sister Florence in the period 1912–13 in connection with her breeding of Egyptian Hunting Dogs (Salukis) at Didlington.[7] The factor common to all these women was a love of the desert, engendered by their travels.

Alicia also sat on other committees connected with her own and Evelyn's interests in the colonies. In 1901–2 Evelyn chaired a select committee on foreign steamship subsidies and was on the executive of the Tariff Reform League from 1903. He wanted to support British trade with the colonies and stop German penetration into East Africa. Alicia was one of Lady Jersey's original committee of the Victoria League in 1901.

'It brought me into contact with Canada and the other Dominions. Evelyn helped to get reduced postage through the House of Commons and to found the Empire Parliamentary Association and the Compatriots' Club; so we were always meeting the chief people, who came for Colonial Conferences and such likes, and entertained many of them in Eaton Place … and from 1914 in Cadogan Square.'[8]

Alicia's work with emigration went on for over forty years – she was not a quitter. It was the same with her work on the Management Council of the Chelsea Physic Garden, a position she held through the nomination of the City Parochial Foundation who had taken over the running of the garden from its founders, the Society of Apothecaries, in 1899. She attended regularly from the first meeting in May 1899 until she resigned on 12 June 1941 during the war, owing to an 'inability to attend future meetings of the Committee because of removal to the country'.[9] Alicia had been appointed because of her strong support for the garden when the Treasury Committee was considering its possible dissolution. She was eminently suited as a garden historian to guide the future of the second oldest botanic garden in England, for she had a great knowledge of ancient herbals and of the functioning of libraries and she lived locally at Eaton Square. She was also very supportive of the current thinking of the City Parochial Foundation as a charity, which had been set up in 1891 to apply funds for 'the poorer classes of the Metropolis'.[10] The purpose was to encourage 'the study of general education, scientific instruction and research in botany including vegetable physiology and instruction in technical pharmacology as far as the culture of medicinal plants is concerned'. The provision of education was then substantially a charitable activity – it was viewed as uplifting the poorer classes. Access to open space was also believed to be health-giving, in both a physical and moral sense, and this was perfectly in accord with the views Alicia expressed in *London Parks and Gardens*. One of the problems of the nineteenth century had been intensely rapid urbanisation. Alicia recognised in the Third Edition of the *History* that 'Nature Study' in the school curriculum 'began with the idea that if a more intelligent appreciation of Nature was impressed on country children, they might be less reluctant to quit the rural districts and crowd into the towns'. Once this had happened, however, the best thing was to ameliorate its worst effects.

Alicia's forty year tenure at the Chelsea Physic Garden coincided both with a period of great investment in its buildings and its glasshouses (which were substantially rebuilt in the first decade of the new century) and with the term of office of one of its greatest Curators, William Hales, who died at the garden in 1937 after 38 years' service. Not much is known about her rôle, however, because the minutes of the CPF meetings are rather more formulaic than enlightening. She regularly made gifts of plants and copies of the *RHS Journal* for the library. She was also involved in the public outcry following the felling of the last of the original four Cedars of Lebanon in 1904 which found expression in a letter to *The Times* on 14th March. Alicia replied to this, explaining 'the circumstances under which the Committee had reluctantly authorised the removal of the tree'.[11] Because of her familiarity with botanical libraries, she was appointed to a Library Sub-Committee which was granted a sum of £25 for the purchase of books.[12] She also requested the Clerk 'to communicate with the Apothecaries Society as to the books and specimens devised by Dr Samuel Dale in 1739, with a view to acquiring them as a nucleus of a Botanical library at the Garden'.[13] Such a library would have been close to Alicia's heart, but it was not to be achieved rapidly. The Apothecaries resisted the removal of books to the Garden and by the end of 1907 'The Committee decided to let the matter drop'.[14] At some stage these 331 books, many of them extremely valuable herbals, were given to the Garden on permanent loan. They became part of the Garden's permanent endowment when its trustees resisted their sale by the Apothecaries and achieved a ruling at the Chancery Bar on 2nd November 1972.[15] Bearing in mind what later happened to the Didlington Library (see page 63), Alicia would have been delighted.

She tried to promote popular botanical lectures at the Garden[16] – in 1916 she successfully obtained facilities for the Herb Growers' Association to give three lectures[17] – and attended many herself: for example, she was recorded as having been present at the Chadwick Trust lectures (which normally attracted 250 people) by Sir Daniel Hall FRS 'On the Sources of the Fruit and Vegetable Supply of London'[18] and on 'Narcotic Plants' by Prof. W.E. Dixon MD, FRS on 7th June 1928. Alicia wrote a chapter on the Chelsea Physic Garden in *London Parks and Gardens* and Hales corresponded with her in March 1904 over the planting date of the *Broussonetia papyrifera* (Paper Mulberry) pictured in her *History*.[19]

Over the years Alicia donated many things to the Garden: a framed photograph of Matthias de L'Obel, two glass negatives of the last of the Old Cedars, an old iron pestle and mortar dated 1649 which her father had purchased in France, and a picture showing the Old Cedar and the river gates at the Garden before the Thames Embankment was constructed.[20] When she resigned, the Committee noted: 'Her cultured interest in, and many benefactions to, the Garden are gratefully recalled by her colleagues. Her classical works on the history of Gardening and on London Parks are highly prized, and her gracious presence was always welcome at the Meetings of the Committee.'[21]

The Chelsea Physic Garden fulfilled many of Alicia's recommendations that green spaces in London should provide education and generate health-giving oxygen for local residents. But its 'parent', the City Parochial Foundation, was also keen to provide culture to the East Enders (they had endowed the Whitechapel Art Gallery in the same year as the Chelsea Physic) and to heal the rift between town and country. In this spirit, Alicia, as their nominee on the council, procured a donation of £5 from the Garden towards the Country in Town Exhibition, held in June 1906 (and again in June 1907 and 1908) at the Gallery. There was an exhibit of the plants grown at Chelsea Physic, augmented by plants taken up by Alicia. She then worked hard at demonstrating the planting of window boxes to thousands of people (see page 47). Lectures were also given (for example, on 'Civic Improvements') under the chairmanship of the prominent Fabian Socialist Sidney Webb. In the *History* she reported that 50,000 people attended the exhibition in a fortnight.

The 'greening' of London which Alicia describes as so important in *London Parks and Gardens* took her into further practical and advisory work. For several years prior to 1909 she was on the Advisory Committee for planting Hampstead Garden Suburb, attending meetings at the house of the instigators of the project, Canon Samuel Barnett and his wife, Henrietta, in Westminster. Like Bedford Park in Chiswick and Ebenezer Howard's town of Letchworth Garden City (both by planner Raymond Unwin), these were experiments in creating an utopian – indeed, Christian – type of urban planning with housing, planting and community facilities integrated in a way which healed the town and country rift.[22] They aimed to encourage neighbourliness and enable different classes to live side by side. The impetus for the Suburb was also close to Alicia's interests: the growth of the railways. Dame Henrietta Barnett, a cosmetics heiress, was keen to preserve land as a northward extension of Hampstead Heath, and the Hampstead Garden Suburb Committee made clear that house rents should be moderate so that working people could live there with gardens and yet reach Central London for the price of a second class train fare. Alicia's planting committee proposed hedges and trellises to divide plots (rather than walls) to 'green' the neighbourhood and was strict about preserving large trees and the two existing woods known as Big Wood and Little Wood. Her expertise was invaluable – Edwin Lutyens, who was involved with Raymond Unwin as a Consulting Architect, rather rudely commented that Henrietta Barnett herself 'had no idea much beyond a window box full of geraniums, calceolarias and lobelias, over which you can see a goose on a green.' The roads were to be tree-lined, 'making where possible, a colour scheme with the hedges', and the houses were to be 50 feet apart 'with gardens occupying the intervening space'. Alicia also supported the Metropolitan Public Gardens Association in a practical way throughout the 1920s until her death by sending up 'bundles of Ponticum Rhododendrons for slum squares and disused churchyards' from the grounds of Lytchett Heath,[23] an idea which would, however, horrify today's conservationists given its invasive habit.

During all this 'good work', and between 1904 and 1908, Alicia was also writing for income as horticultural correspondent for *The Times*, reporting on the major flower shows. She described it as 'a business and often very amusing'.[24]

> I was regularly employed by *The Times* to report on all important flower shows (I did this quite well paid interesting work for over four years when I had to give up for illness); the RHS Colonial Fruit, National Rose, National Chrysanthemum Shows … sometimes I had amusing adventures as, known to be a keen gardener, no one thought it odd that I should be to the fore at shows, but they little suspected that I was writing for *The Times* … I did a good deal of reviewing too, very amusing work and well paid too …[25]

Why earning money was so important to her in this period is not certain. But in 1906 the Amhersts suffered a huge financial catastrophe and it is possible that Alicia felt the need to assist her father. This awful event was, in its time, as significant as the ruin of Barings Bank by the trader Nick Leeson. The family were later to name it 'The Deluge'.

8

The Deluge

As with many wealthy families, it was the habit of the Amhersts to spend a great part of the British winter and spring in the south of France. Two years after their grand trip to Egypt, in February 1897, the Amhersts and four of their daughters (Sib, Flo, Maggie and Alicia) left to join May, her husband Willy and their sons at Valescure, two miles inland from St Raphael. They rented accommodation, the Villa Clythia. It was an idyllic, prolonged, holiday existence: 'Wed 24th Sketched the aloes near the bridge on Fréjus road am, afternoon the whole party in carriages and on bykes out to the quarries where the Romans got the stone for the Aquaduct. On the Bagnol road about 3½ kilometre beyond Fréjus. So hot I byke with parasol up.' The 26th was another 'lovely hot day'; they went by train to Cannes to arrange 'to hire for a month a nice looking little boat called the "Coulis"', lunched at the Hotel Splendide, shopped, returned by train and then 'up to the Villa La Maquis to tea with the Halls'.

Nice is well known for its spring carnival and on 2nd March they went to the town with a cold Mistral wind blowing and bought the boys Pierrot suits. After lunching at the Terminus Hotel they joined the carnival at 2.00p.m.: 'We pelted and were pelted with showers of confetti without one minutes pause until we left the stand at 4.30.' The parade had a 'torpedo and sailors, a bull fight, a huge fan, a great fish … a giraffe with boys holding onto his neck etc., all very good' and the boys 'looked such ducks as Pierots [*sic*]'.

An excursion by train to Grasse took place on 6th March, from which they returned with 'quantities of violets'; on 7th Alicia sketched some umbrella pines with a view of Fréjus while 'Maggie and Willy took the boys to tea on the Coulis in the harbour'. The next day they visited a cork manufacturing plant in Bagnol 'and Sib cut some corks'. Unfortunately, illness struck between 13th and 26th when Sib and May got flu, prompting Alicia's comment: 'It seems a fate that whenever we are abroad one of our party at least gets ill' (perhaps remembering the death of her younger sister, Bea, at Cannes in 1881). As Sib's temperature rose from 95° to 105.6° there was much concern to stop the infection spreading. On 18th 'Fardie [Alicia's affectionate name for the father] and I went in the Coulis to Cap Canarard & went up the lighthouse & got a dusting coming back. It was a lovely full moon & the rough sea in a mistral squall looked lovely.' Continuing the social scene, 'Mother and Maggie went to Mentone to see Kate and Willy Mitford and stayed with them the night at the Splendide Hotel and lunched at Monte Carlo next day.' On 26th Alicia took her nephew, Jacky, out on a lovely warm day 'and picked Cistus and Bee orchids and lupins on the hills'.

On 19th May the villa rental ended and the party split up, some to return to England by train via the Italian lakes. Alicia, her mother, Flo and Sib went by train to Avignon. Sib had recovered by 27th but Alicia's temperature rose to 102.2° and she was treated with quinine which seemed to effect a cure. They stayed in Aix-les-Bains to allow Lady Amherst to take 'douches' for her back pain. This enabled Alicia to take advantage of her friendship with Ellen Willmott at her nearby villa, 'Tresserve': 'We have had a nice time and some lovely excursions. Miss Willmott & her sister & brother-in-law Robert Berkeley have been most kind and helped to arrange excursions.'[1]

These idyllic holidays in the south of France eventually prompted Lord Amherst to build a very substantial villa there rather than rent accommodation yearly. He had to purchase land first and the solicitor he used was the firm of Cheston at 1 Winchester Street Buildings, London E6. Lord Amherst used the youngest son, Charles, in whom he had great faith. We know his opinion of him from an introduction he wrote to Percy Newberry on 7th December 1900 when Cheston was planning a visit to Egypt: 'You may have a visit from Mr Cheston. I think you have met him at Didlington. He is my Family Solicitor and manages all my Hackney Estates. He is a good scholar himself as far as University Education goes and a very pleasant companion. I am keen you will do all you can to give him an insight into the wonders of Upper Egypt.'[2]

The villa, subsequently named 'Lou Casteou', was built on a rise at

111.08 metres north of St Raphael in his beloved Valescure. The architect was Henri Lacreusette and the dwelling bore more than a passing
resemblance to Didlington having an Italianate tower. It was to be three
storeys, entered via a covered archway into a formal enclosed courtyard.
The façade faced the sea, and was decorated with a large painted
sundial. Lord Amherst laid the foundation stone which bore his family
crest on 30th May 1903 and made a brief speech:

> It is with feelings of very great pleasure that I place the first stone of this
> house. For 7 years I have known Valescure, and every year I love it more
> and more, therefore to have a home of my own here has been one of my
> greatest wishes, but many circumstances have combined to make it imposs-
> ible until now. It seems rather presumptuous to begin to build a house at
> our age [he was 68] but I hope we may all be spared to come here for a few
> more years to enjoy this lovely spot and that it will be a joy to those who
> may follow us.[3]

His speech was bitterly prescient, for the Amhersts were to be spared
only a few more years. In June 1906, while at 'Lou Casteou', the family
heard of the death by suicide of Charles Cheston amid rumours of
financial misdealing.

The subsequent newspaper reports of the financial scandal do not
give nearly as vivid or complete a record of what the family later called
'The Deluge', as does Alicia's own account:

> It was gambling on the stock exchange which ruined him. His fortnightly
> settlements amounted to over 100,000 – when he got desperate he just
> robbed all his clients, took all the trust monies he could lay hands on and
> plunged deeper into speculation … the second son (was) as great a rogue as
> his father. He was able during the time which elapsed between Cheston's
> death and our finding out it was suicide, to destroy papers and do all he
> could to hide all traces of the guilt. It is horrible to think of his smiling,
> deferential pleasant manner, all the time concealing so much craft. I think it
> must have started in a small way and got deeper and deeper until he saw he
> must be shown up. He wrote his own obituary notice and poisoned himself,
> after playing a game of bridge and saying goodnight to his wife (who, by the
> way, drank), and that he had some business to finish. I hate even to feel
> someone one knew so well and was so often in contact with [could be capa-
> ble of] such crime. The harm he did will never be estimated as the hardship,
> sorrow and worry he caused to so many families had such far reaching

consequences. The crash had come just at the time of my father and mother's golden wedding. They intended to return from Valescure just before the 4th June 1906 and we looked forward to fetes and celebrations at Didlington. They knew of the disaster just before and lingered in France, as they were motoring home. Evelyn went to meet them at Dieppe and explain some of the details they had not heard …[4]

The degree of ruin that the Amhersts faced was not immediately evident. As the news spread, so did the outrage:

I am horrified at what Margaret's letter this morning tells me about Cheston's outrageous dishonesty and appalling robbery … it is a most difficult thing to discover a clever thief and there seems no doubt that both you and I have been outrageously deceived. I heard that his estate was proved the other day at £37,000 – which I presume we can claim as an asset. I feel so upset I cannot write more now.[5]

Gradually, as the extent of the fraud was revealed, the Amhersts sold assets to meet the debts, starting with their London home at 8, Grosvenor Square, then selling pictures from Didlington. Howard Carter, on a visit home at Fyvie Castle in Aberdeenshire, wrote forlornly to Newberry: 'Didlington is in brown paper parcels and Lady Amherst saving odd bits of string.'[6] Lord Amherst put on a brave face for his daughters but Alicia was clear about the real effect it had on him:

'The Deluge' came as a dark cloud on our happy life. Father never minded the actual poverty. He said to me once when walking around the lake at Didlington at the end of July when we began to realise the extent of the crash, 'One must not mind as it is *only* money! There was no disgrace, no loss of loved ones, only loss of things and comforts. We did not know then all the cost, really in spite of his philosophy and of the heroic calm with which 'daddens' bore everything, it caused his death … In spite of all his calm resignation, the strain and worry of the sales and the awful amount of the debt, could not fail to try him mentally and physically. He felt most of all the perfidy of Cheston. He had known him all his life – the father had been the lawyer when father had succeeded in 1856 and there had been an elder brother of the wicked Charles Cheston called William who had died years before who father had been very fond of, and also younger brothers – the chief favourite … was Charles and gradually more and more had been confided to him. He was made 'Steward of the Manor of Hackney' and that gave him opportunities to be fraudulent. His manner was always pleasant and open and not at all like a villain – and we were not the only people taken in by him …

Immediately, Alicia set about trying to arrange for the sale of her father's library 'complete', and she wrote an account of the books in the interests of keeping them together – 'Father had collected them not haphazard but as a sequence, each section complete in itself.' There was not only the history of printing, the history of the Reformation in England and the English Bibles but also the gardening books and herbals which she had collected and books concerning the voyages of discovery. To these were added histories of Freemasonry and the history of the Order of St John of Jerusalem (of which her father was a Knight of Justice and, later, Evelyn, was Secretary right through the 1st World War). Alicia recounted that '… notes on the books were sent to Liverpool [University] who at one time contemplated purchase and great hopes were held out by Montreal and I met Dr Osler who was sent by them to inspect the books in the safes in the city where they were stored. That visit was the last occasion on which I handled many of the beloved volumes …'[7]

The Amhersts enlisted all their social contacts to help sell the collection complete. On 11th June 1907 Lady Amherst wrote to Newberry (by then Professor of Egyptology at the University of Liverpool): '… you know how valuable the books are, and how perfect each series is. Though *we* might perhaps make more money by dividing them, they could never be so perfect a collection for the purchaser, as the collection now is, as a *whole* … so many [genuine treasures] have already gone to America, England's chance of such a thing is rather exceptional and *really* worth considering.'[8] Nowadays, such an important collection would probably have been bought for the nation by the Heritage Lottery Fund or the National Heritage Memorial Fund.

Alicia also wrote to Newberry with further details: 'The matter is more pressing than ever as we must have £20,000 by June 30th and may have to sell some of the gems out of the library and let the rest go to auction later.'[9] She hoped he would effect an introduction to the wealthy businessman Carnegie. But it was not to be and the famous library that had given birth to the book which started the discipline of garden history in England was split up. On 9th October Lady Amherst wrote to Newberry from Didlington:

We are very shortly to move away from here though I am sorry to say we have not yet let the house and now I fear it is too late this year. We have to sell all the precious books. Quaritch came to value them and our hope is they realise a good sum. We shall be able to put 'straight' again in time but the fraud has been so gigantic that we can hardly realise it all. We have frantically shut up the house and have got places for nearly all our old servants. Our horses are all gone, it is fortunate that we bought a motor last year. Our red poll cattle are sold, and our farm is let ... Books being packed up and taken to London ... Quaritch of course will manage all that for us ...[10]

The family moved to Foulden Hall, a brick built property on the Didlington Estate. The manor of Foulden had belonged to Francis Tyssen from 1770, and, luckily, had been transferred to Lady Amherst as part of her marriage settlement in May 1868 – ironically by the firm of Cheston, and therefore was not under constraint of sale.[11] Alicia, also busy at the time with the proofs and picture permissions for *London Parks and Gardens*, received many good wishes about the family's predicament. From the Keeper of the Privy Purse at Sandringham, after giving His Majesty's permission to report on Buckingham Palace Garden: 'I am so sorry for your father and all of you, that you have to look out for a tenant for Didlington, and as such is the case, I trust you may be able to find a good one, who will keep the house in its present perfect order during, I hope only a short stay, he or she, will have to be there.' And from Lord Redesdale, along with information about London's parks and gardens while he was in charge of the Office of Works: 'I was so very sorry to hear about your father's worries – such a heavy blow! I am afraid the loss of the library will be a misery to him.'[12] There was also sympathy from the other end of the social scale – from ex-workers on the Didlington Estate like James Trimbee who had been Second Journeyman in the greenhouses from February 1902, in charge of the Orchard House and later the great displays of chrysanthemums. He described hearing of Cheston's suicide with a heavy heart, 'the high standing of the Amherst family and the many generations of family servants all ruined by the greed of one man'.[13] The amount lost by Lord Amherst was estimated at £250,000 but it was not the total of his losses. With a Captain Dowler he was a trustee of the estate of the late Andrew Fountaine; Fountaine's daughter, Mary, and her son, Charles, brought an action in the Chancery Division for the loss of nearly £70,000 (or three-quarters of the Fountaine Estate funds). Lord Justice Warrington declared in favour of the Fountaines, so this debt was added to Lord Amherst's woes.

In the subsequent sales Lord Amherst, aided especially by Alicia, tried to make good. In a speech at a public lunch at Marham, Norfolk, he was reported 'under the stress of evident emotion' as wishing

> ... to take this opportunity which you kindly have given me by inviting me here of thanking my friends from the bottom of my heart – for the very great sympathy which you have shown us in this cruel financial trouble which has so suddenly come upon us in our old age. The trouble is, indeed, a cruel and heavy one. But I have every reason to hope that by the necessary strict economy and very great sacrifices we may be able to pull our affairs round, so that we may live amongst you after a year or two.[14]

The subsequent sales at Sotheby's and Christie's were attended by Lord Amherst 'with one of his daughters', where he appeared 'as cheerful and calm as if he had been buying instead of selling'.[15] Clearly he was trying to maximise the sum raised as a matter of honour rather than from some misplaced desire to punish himself. The following newspaper report sketched the scene after his death:

> In a long and varied experience of art and literary sales at auction, nothing more pathetic has been witnessed by the hardened market than the recent Amherst dispersals at Sotheby's and Christie's. The late peer loved his treasures as part and parcel of himself and it was only the highest sense of duty which urged him to disperse them, in order to meet the demands made on him by the malpractices of a trusted agent. Yet it was evident that he found some form of relief in attending the auction funeral of his cherished books and objets d'art. Day by day he sat at Sotheby's and Christie's and watched the market deposit wreaths upon his treasures. Now and again he would let a little exclamation of disappointment escape from him as some book of rare (but forgotten) erudition – which he knew from beginning to end – went for a comparatively small sum, yet, on the whole, he derived a vast satisfaction from the market's reception. As stated at the time in the columns, he was especially delighted with the German 'Graduale's' fate. This manuscript, he gleefully informed one representative, had cost him only £60, and it was the first of its kind which he had bought from Bernard Quaritch the elder, who had offered to buy it back from him for £600. On

the sale day it fetched £1,650, given by Mr Quaritch the younger, in the teeth of a strong Continental attack.[16]

Fifteen Caxton Bibles were sold to Pierpont Morgan in America. Louis Quinze Gobelins furniture together with rare Limoges enamels brought the Christie's total to £26,000. His tapestries were withdrawn at his reserve in an attempt to reach a higher price.

Lord Amherst died shortly after these sales at 23, Queen's Gate Gardens in London after an illness of only a few hours on 6th January 1909. He was buried in Didlington Church, a memorial service being held at St George's, Hanover Square, the scene in 1898 of Alicia's wedding.

The following year, on 29th November 1910, also in Hanover Square at the rooms of Knight, Frank & Rutley, was auctioned his old home of Didlington Hall and the 7,105 acres of the Didlington estate. The auction catalogue held in the Norfolk County Records Office reveals the Hall as having 12 reception rooms, 46 bedrooms with 5 dressing rooms and 7 bathrooms, all with electric light and centrally heated. It was sold with stabling for 16 horses, coach houses and motor garages, cottages for gardeners, coachmen and electrician, a kitchen garden with vineries, a model laundry, two entrance lodges and a private cricket ground, 60 acres of lakes and a park of 700 acres with 1,000 acres of woodland, the greater part of Foulden and Ickburgh villages, 16 farms, cottages, the White Hart Inn at Foulden and a Water Mill at Northwold. Alicia was too ill to attend.

The purchaser was a Colonel Smith. Alicia later noted that the *Amherstia* in the Special Plant House in the Kitchen Garden came to a sad end: 'our's flowered year after year most beautifully until 1908 when we thought Didlington might have to be sold. It just died. We felt it would not live with strangers.'[17] A bitter departure indeed.

9

Out of Action, then War Work

Between 1908 and 1911 letters both from and to Alicia mention that she was not in good health – it became a continuous refrain. Walter S. Ledger on 5th June 1908 commented 'you mention you are not in good health.' Another letter from a friend staying at the Villa d'Este at Cernobbio on Lake Como on 16th May 1909 noted she was better but 'you must have had such a weary time of it these last 15 months being so ill, I saw you had had to leave your London house [she was staying at Hansell Manor, Eridge, Sussex]. I hope your native air may help you to get strong again.' Whatever the problem was it was having a prolonged effect and seriously restricting what she could do and whom she could meet: 'some day if I am well enough I should much like to see you' she wrote to Lord Curzon on 23rd January 1911.[1] She had given up working as a horticultural correspondent for *The Times*.

Alicia described what happened to her in her *Notes on my life and family for my children* written, with extraordinarily detailed remembrance, in 1941. The trouble began shortly after she and Evelyn had spent their tenth wedding anniversary at Bisham Abbey.

> How little did I think I should not walk home from church for 5 long years!! It is lucky the future is hidden! It was on our 15th anniversary of our wedding day that I was next able to walk to church service and back again! When we got home to London we discovered that Nanny Alders had collapsed with influenza suddenly – Saturday evening … I kept all the children away. Next morning she was better – it was a short and sharp attack. I went on to a Victoria League meeting at 11, suddenly when I was driving home with Mrs Ennett, in a hansom, I said I felt ill and found I had caught flu! I went straight to bed as soon as I got in. Dr Waugh arrived and found the evil germ had gone to my heart and I was made to lie absolutely still.

This was the beginning of years of illness. After about six weeks [I was told] to lie absolutely still for about three months. I remember how kindly everyone sympathised. How trying it would be for anyone *so active* to be still for three whole months! At the end of three years I was still being told the same thing but luckily could not see so far ahead …

If her doctor was correct, she was suffering from inflammation of the heart muscle caused by the influenza virus – 'influenzal myocarditis'. This is a serious and sometimes fatal illness. She described her symptoms thus: 'suffered frightfully from headaches as well as the other tiresome heart symptoms, breathlessness and feeling as if one was going to faint away to nothing when one is lying still … I struggled to get better but seemed only to get worse. When in London, as I could not walk upstairs, I slept in a tiny room on the ground floor …' These are all consistent with myocarditis, except the headaches.[2] But Alicia had other reasons for headaches: she must have been extraordinarily stressed by 'The Deluge' and the continuing need to support her father.[3] Furthermore, she was still finalising *London's Parks and Gardens*.

In June 1908 she was taken to Ripley in Surrey and then Ockham to spend nine weeks in a cottage there with a resident nurse. Evelyn used to visit and once brought the children to see her. That Christmas they went to Lytchett – '… and it was while I was there that daddens died quite suddenly in London. He and mother had come up from Foulden the day before and to stay for a few days … before going to Valescure … we knew his heart was weak … I was far too ill [to go back]. It was on Jan 6th 1909 and he never regained consciousness.'

Ill fortune seemed to pile on ill fortune and she felt that her father-in-law, Eustace Cecil, lacked understanding while she was at Lytchett. 'I could not eat much and had to sit through long dinners … I had a nurse who came from London and stayed a night twice a week and gave me Nauheim treatment and I began to feel a little better …' Nauheim treatment was a water cure much favoured in the spas of Germany whither Alicia travelled on several occasions to receive it. In autumn 1909 she remembered seeing 'the balloon like airship, the first I ever saw, flying in the sky on 15th Sept. 1909 and on Sept. 21st I actually saw Zeppelin 3 with Count Zeppelin himself over Nauheim … and the whole town turned out to see it fly over en route for Frankfurt.' Little was she to know that these Zeppelins were to claim 1,500 lives by bombing Britain in the coming Great War.

Then it was back to Lytchett for Christmas and to Nauheim again for further treatment in spring 1910. These treatments seemed to do some good, but life was still about a mixture of celebration and loss:

> We all met up at Foulden on my return and ... I was able to go about with the children and friends ... The great event of my visit was Auntie May and Uncle Willie's silver wedding – I was taken in by bath chair to Didlington to watch the festivities and the children stayed up to see the amateur fireworks. I stayed the night at Didlington and little thought it was the last time in my old home. The 2nd September 1910 was their silver wedding and we went to Lytchett to be in time for the golden wedding of grandmama and grandpapa on Sept. 18th.

At the beginning of May 1911 Evelyn went house-hunting. He found a suitable place near Haslemere in Surrey and rented a London flat at 36, Buckingham Gate. In August 1911 she and the children moved from Foulden to Haslemere, with the old coachman from Lytchett to look after them. They used a donkey to pull her bathchair, which must have reminded her of her youth at Didlington. Alicia relates that, after a year there

> ... we heard of a German doctor, Dr Grodick, and as I was still so ill we decided to consult him. In the end I started off at his clinique in Baden in August 1912. Evelyn travelled with me. I had to be carried off the train ... my friend Elizabeth Northcote was a patient too. It certainly is the most dramatic treatment and was nearly three months before I showed any signs of improvement. The doctor gave violent massage and hot bath, one day only the arms and the next day legs, and the third day sitting in the water covered. The water was kept at 116°F for 20 mins. In November when I returned with Elsie Northcote I was able to walk quite briskly on and off the steamer ... I made a second visit to Baden in 1913–14 ... How little we could have dreamed that we should have been at war in less than 10 months.

Alicia was lucky. She had recovered her health in time to get out of Germany before the war. Her elder sister May and husband Willy were not so lucky. They were trapped there at the outbreak of war and had to 'use influence' to get out.

Gradually, Alicia regained her strength. Soon she was able to help Mags with nursing wounded troops, and, by 1917, even to take on ten hour days of war work for the production of food.

Alicia herself was partly involved in nursing during the war, along with sisters Florence and Magsie; the latter was Commandant of a Red Cross/St John's Voluntary Aid Detachment hospital at Buckenham Tofts Hall, Mundford, Norfolk between 1916 and 1917. This was obvious war work for the sisters who were all Dames of Grace of the Order of St John of Jerusalem, a branch of the original Knights of Malta, whose members had fought in The Crusades and formed an order of chivalry both Military and Hospitaller in its ethos (for the knights also tended the sick and injured). Alicia describes serving in 'Magsie's St John's Hospital, [where] I found myself nursing a Boer who had lost his leg. To cheer him, I talked of places in South Africa and found he might have been one of the men who booed at us at Potchefstram. He told me that was the day he joined his Commando to go to Natal.' She felt that when war was declared, in 1914, 'the trust we had put in the Boers, was amply justified.' The kindness of all the sisters to the wounded men was notable. They even sent braces of pheasant to them when they returned home. Typical also, is a comment from Alicia: 'Do you realise Gladys Howlett who has been 2nd housemaid at Lytchett is going to marry Frank Barfoot wounded soldier and son of Barfoot the gardener – she is at home now. Could you find out if she wants her present from me (a thing I hear she wanted [was] a tapestry table cloth) sent to Foulden or Lytchett – I want to know before I go to Lytchett Friday.'[4]

Alicia was involved in more war work from 1917 to 1919, though this was in the crucial area of food production rather than nursing. The background to her contribution is interesting, not least because it parallels some of today's discussion about 'food security'. On 17th June 1915 a parliamentary committee had been set up under Lord Selborne as President of the Board of Agriculture and Fisheries, under the chairmanship of Viscount Milner 'on the assumption that the war may be prolonged beyond the harvest of 1916, to consider and report what steps should be taken by legislation or otherwise for the sole purpose of maintaining and if possible increasing the present production of food in England and Wales'. In its final report of 15th October 1915 the Milner Committee, noting that two-thirds of Britain's food was imported 'from countries outside the British Empire' gave its opinion that:

a State purchasing the greater part of its food from foreign sources is *ipso facto* more open to attack and in a more unstable economic position when war comes. We hope therefore, that the importance of bringing our poorer pastures under arable cultivation will be recognised by the Government and the agricultural community. In our opinion, it is only on these lines that a substantial increase in our home production of food can be achieved.

The committee also recommended an increase in pig keeping, not allowing skilled farm workers to enlist and, instead, 'an appeal on patriotic grounds to women ... to offer their services to local farmers'. Local education authorities and county committees should offer training, as should the Women's Farm and Garden Union, and wages for women on piece-work should be the same as men. They further recommended the use of waste land in villages and suburbs for the production of vegetables, land being compulsorily purchased, if necessary, under the Small Holdings and Allotments act; all the above to be organised through War Food Societies.[5] In many ways, this was the forerunner of the 'Dig for Victory' campaign of World War II and the Women's Land Army.

On 7th March 1917 H. Eustace Davies, the General Secretary to the Board of Agriculture and Fisheries (Food Production Department) wrote to the Secretary of the Treasury to ask for more help with extra staff for the Department owing to increased work. To help his case he noted that they had also recruited volunteers: 'The Board have been fortunate in obtaining the gratuitous assistance of a number of experts of the highest standing for dealing with the problem of food production ...'[6] One of these was Alicia. Just as her social connections had got her into private gardens and archives while researching her *History*, so too they sent her straight to the top of the pile of potential volunteers:

It was only natural that, knowing Roland Prothero (Lord Ernlie) head of the Ministry of Agriculture in the last [Boer] war, and Lord Lee of Fareham, who was made head of the Food Production department, that [*sic*] they should ask me to help.

In January 1917 I was made Honorary Assistant Director of Horticulture, Dr Frederick Keeble being my Chief. We got on very well together and I put in some 10 hours every day till 1919. My first day, in large offices in Victoria Street, Dr Keeble and I met for the first time and discussed plans, apparently none had been made, and everything had to be evolved. He was full of ideas and practical knowledge and we knew the RHS would help.

Alicia's knowledge of gardening and her organising abilities were to become vital:

Soon, my share of the work was to help the allotment-holders, all over the kingdom, to produce more food. We were shorter than anyone knew, in 1917. I was to get capable gardeners in rural and urban districts and to aim at getting a thousand who would help to advise and organise the allotment-holders. They were called Horticultural Representatives and the only pay they had was the right to claim up to £2 for out of pocket expenses and very few claimed as much as this.

We got many Clubs started, so that the men could get their seeds and tools in larger quantities and share them. It was often my job to see that they did get them – especially seed potatoes. I don't remember where all the secretaries, voluntary and paid, came from, but they all appeared; the whole place was buzzing. Sir John Arkwright was helpful finding voluntary workers. I remember one voluntary worker, the owner, I believe, of immense stores of Tea in bond, who came and most humbly wrote letters for me two days a week.

She was prepared to do anything to promote the goal, including being media-savvy:

There were sometimes funny incidents; potato disease was much feared and a knapsack sprayer had been produced cheaply to try and persuade people to spray. One morning, one of Dr Keeble's secretaries rushed into my room to ask if I would come immediately with him in a taxi to be photographed spraying potatoes in Hyde Park, near the Albert Memorial. I walked up and down with the sprayer on my back, while photos were being taken. I never saw them, though they appeared in all the papers next day.

Another time, Dr Keeble asked me if I could help him to get the King to allow the photo to be taken of vegetables in his garden, being sent to hospitals, as we were trying to organise better supplies for the hospitals. I rang up Derek Keppel and explained to him – within a few minutes he was able to get to the King who at once gave permission.

But above all, it was what we would now call her 'networking' ability which oiled the wheels and delivered the results, as with the need for Vitamin C in the nation's diet:

When the blackberry season was coming on, Dr Keeble wanted to try to organise schoolchildren to pick in five counties, which he thought would be most prolific in England. He was having difficulty with the Board of Education, as to what day the children should be allowed to pick. It seemed ridiculous to make a hard and fast rule, when that particular day might be wet. Dr Keeble was very fussed. I knew Sir Amherst Selby Bigg [sic] was the head of the Education Department, so I promised to see what I could do and solemnly got through to him, as Honorary Assistant Director of Horti-culture, speaking from the Food Production Department. I gave him a shock by saying: 'Is that you, Doddles?' When I made myself known, we very soon settled the whole question. The collection was so successful, it was done on a much larger scale in 1918.[7]

Like so many people in the war, Alicia found that working together for a common cause produced great satisfaction over the practical results:

I remember one morning the town clerk of a large Yorkshire town, Wakefield, Macclesfield, arriving with a map; it was spread out on my table while he consulted me where he was to plant potatoes. After some practical cross-questioning, I settled on four places on the four sides of the town and promised that within three days I would send him an expert gardener to advise on each spot and see that he got the potato seed. I thought no more about it, but many months later, the same town clerk was announced. He said he had business in London and had just called in, as he thought I would like to know that the hour spent over his map had produced 30 tons of potatoes.

As it was in London, so it was at Lytchett where all the children's garden plots were turned over to vegetable production but with a typical Alicia twist. They were planted ornamentally, with tall sweet corn at the centre of the bed, then cabbages, and carrots around the outside; sunflowers were justified at the back of the borders on the grounds that the seeds were nourishing. This must have been a solace to Maud, Alicia's youngest daughter, who was lonely during the war with her mother in London, her sister nearly grown up and her brother at board-ing school.[8] Like so many women in the war, Alicia found her experi-ences exciting because she was having success:

I could tell many incidents. One more I must not forget. The War Savings Department asked us to organise the collection in our office, when one of the first Tanks on view was in Trafalgar Square, and said they would send a carrier pigeon to bring a cheque to the tank if £200 was raised. Four days before the allotted time, I put up notices all over our offices to say we had got as much as £180, and hoped a great effort would be made as I had ordered the pigeon. I was astonished by the excitement all through the office, from my Horticultural van girls above and the tractors below. By the actual day we had raised £1,200. Lord Lee came to my room to let off the pigeon. The traffic was stopped and the whole of the department stood in the street to watch the pigeon circle round, and then fly off to the tank.

In the spring of 1918 she was recognised for her success in this important (but voluntary) role with the award of MBE:

It caused immense delight in the Department. If one of the Brownie messengers or the Lift attendant had had it, there could hardly have been more excitement. When I came back from the Palace, wearing the Silver Cross, they all crowded round me. I gave it to be shown throughout the office and was astonished how pleased they were. Some other official got it, too, and we walked together to Buckingham Palace.

The King was only in a small room and it was all very informal. When he saw me coming up to him, he said in the most cheery manner: 'What am I giving you this for?' I said, 'For helping to grow potatoes and cabbages.' He, at once, laughing said, 'Well, I am glad for once they have put a round peg in a round hole – I know how much you know about it!' and gave me a warm handshake, when he put on the Cross.[9]

In 1920 this was upgraded to CBE.

It is hard to avoid the view that, for Alicia, the experience of the war was distinctly therapeutic. However, it did not leave the Amhersts or the Cecils untouched. Alicia lost her much-loved nephew Billy, of the Grenadier Guards, within a month of the start of hostilities, and nephew Tommy lost a leg. On 2nd November 1919 her mother died and was buried at All Saint's Church, Foulden. But, as Britain entered the 1920s, Alicia's life was about to change yet again.

10

Lytchett Heath – A Garden at Last

In 1921 Lord Eustace Cecil, Evelyn's father, died and left his son
Lytchett Heath. Evelyn and Alicia were to live there permanently there-
after. During the war, when Alicia had been working on food production, Evelyn had been working hard to rein in public finance as a
member of the Committee on Public Retrenchment set up in 1915. He
was also busy doing charitable work as Secretary-General of the Order
of St John of Jerusalem from 1915–1921 and it was this effort which
gained him a knighthood in January 1922. In the 1920s Alicia largely
abandoned writing (except for a few articles) in favour of a combination
of busy charitable work and recreating and extending the garden at
Lytchett.

Lord Eustace Cecil had had the house built in 1873 and modelled it
closely on the architectural style of Hatfield House. The site was a
meadow of infertile grassland, oat fields and heathland with two conical
hills scattered with Scotch firs planted around 1750. There were a few
hollies, hedgerow elm and a valley with a stream to the west, wooded
with oaks. His gardener was Charles Cox who arrived in October 1878
and was only to retire after fifty years. During the years 1875–79 they
had planted a great quantity of trees, particularly conifers such as *Pinus
radiata*, the Monterey Pine, which self-sowed itself, *Cupressus macrocarpa*
which attained a huge height and girth, *Picea smithiana* and *Cedrus atlantica*
grown from a cone collected by Lord Eustace in Lebanon in 1869.
Lytchett soon became a repository for seed sent back by Lord Eustace
and his son Evelyn from their foreign travels, including their military
service. They became keen plant collectors, one of their earliest
despatches being a cutting from the willow on Napoleon's grave,
collected in 1852 on Lord Eustace's way to the Cape with his regiment.

Wellingtonia seed was sent from Mariposa Grove in California and *Pinus thunbergii, Cryptomeria japonica elegans, Juniperus chinensis,* the Lacquer Tree *Rhus vernicifera* and maples were all sent back from Japan in 1887. This accorded with the Victorian love of evergreens, particularly conifers, and most did well in the unpolluted Dorset air – so well that it became Alicia's and Evelyn's job to reduce them to maintain the views south-wards of Poole Harbour, the Purbeck Hills, Corfe Castle and the Arne peninsula.

Alicia saw herself as part of this great plant hunting and gardening tradition: '… the habit of bringing home floral souvenirs from many parts of the world has been continued. Lord Eustace welcomed novel-ties which Sir Evelyn and I found on our travels, and many were firmly established during his lifetime.' In 1931, she reminisced:

> The latest additions to the garden are type tulips dug up by our son, Robert, in Kurdistan last June. The cypress I collected on the Mount of Olives has been standing out since 1898 and has not suffered during any hard winters. The greenhouse, too, has had many contributions from overseas. In 1899 my husband and I collected and delivered specimens for Kew in Southern Rhodesia and in a few weeks found no fewer than forty new species. The showy Haemanthus Cecilae has flowered well but once, and is no more, but a new variety of Gloriosa, named by Mr Baker of Kew from our dried specimen, G. superba lutea, is a joy every year.[1]

Alicia must have felt very at home in a heathland garden with large conifers. In that respect it was like Didlington – but without the huge lakes and vast Norfolk skies – and, of course, not flat. But it did have a south-facing aspect and Dorset was a much milder county which made it an ideal location to experiment with hardiness. Many eucalypts were tried including, *E. whittingehamensis, E. urnigera, E. globulus, E. ficifolia, E. buneri, E. obliqua, E. calophylla* and *E.macarthurii,* which succeeded, but *E. regnans, E. pauciflora* and *E. stringei* were all killed outright in 1929. Other Australian species she tried were *Clianthus puniceus magnificus,* which she also lost in 1929, and various acacias. *Acacia dealbata,* the mimosa, grew to 25 feet but was killed in 1923, though later succeeded against a wall; *Acacia affinis* grew well, while *A. longifolia* and *A. melanoxy-lon* grew back after frost damage, but she failed with *A. baileyana* and *A. floribunda.* 1917 seemed to be a bad year for she lost a huge *Pittisporum tobira* and all her tree ferns (*Dicksonia antarctica*) but the Bottlebrush, *Callistemon speciosus*, and the Chilean Fire Tree, *Embothrium coccineum*, all recovered. 1929–30 was better and gazanias overwintered.

For many years, at least from 1903 onwards, Alicia corresponded with a succession of Directors of the Royal Botanic Gardens, Kew, over the great wonder of Lytchett, its tree heather cover. In 1931 she wrote: 'The most remarkable feature of the whole garden is Erica lusitanica' which flowered in such quantities that it was cut yearly and bunched and boxed for sale in London [an activity in which, according to photographs now at Lytchett, Alicia participated herself]. This had been planted by Lord Eustace and had spread over several acres by seed, some attaining a height of fifteen feet.

> They [are] both best at about 6 to 8 feet, when on a January day they are a mass of white flowers and pink buds. After a very hot summer, such as 1921 or 1928, it is in bloom by November, and full out by Christmas, but in most years from January to April it is at its best … The path to the Chapel of St Aldhelm, which Lord Eustace built in the grounds in 1897, is for 300 yards banked on either side by E. lusitanica, which is specially attractive when, as is often the case, the walk to church on Christmas Day is between walls of white blooms.[2]

Alicia was keen to experiment with other species of heath. On 7th February 1903 she wrote to Kew's Director, Sir William Dyer, offering to lend her father's index of the *Botanical Magazine* which Quaritch had published in 1883 and ended, 'The Erica codonodes at Lytchett has been beautiful this year and all the heaths you sent are doing well.'[3] Sir William sent more plants and on 12th November 1905 Alicia wrote to thank him:

> Lord Eustace was quite astonished at the size of the crate & its varied contents. I spent a delightful morning unpacking yesterday but a wet afternoon prevented much planting. Lord Eustace is specially pleased with the hybrid Erica (arborea x lusitanica). I was very much interested in seeing the way the Kew heaths are propagated, & hope to experiment with profit to the garden here … It is still wonderfully wild here. The large verbena bushes outside the windows not out yet … I trust some day you will see some of these other heaths seeding all about the lusitanica.[4]

Sir William did visit Lytchett and became a friend, and Alicia would keep him updated on interesting flowerings. All her married life she mingled travel and botanical exploration with support for her husband's work. 'I have just been down to Lytchett,' she wrote to Dyer:

> ... on our return from America and found one of the bulbs we brought back from Natal 5 years ago in flower. Dierama pendula. I think it is not often flowered. I fear it is already over, but I thought I would tell you. It was figured as you no doubt know as Sparaxis pendula in Bot. mg: 1830, but the flowers I saw in Natal were a brilliant pink and far more graceful than that plate. [She offered it for the *Magazine* another year.] We had a most interesting tour from a flower, as well as a railway point of view. We were at Montreal in Canada and into Mexico and saw the Grand Cañon in Arizona, so we covered a wide country.[5]

Alicia's enchantment with Lytchett extended beyond plant collecting into garden design from 1900 onwards when, one year after her marriage, Lord Eustace let her select a spot for her own 'special garden'. Lytchett Heath had south and west facing terraces around the house, then a bank planted with *Rhododendron ponticum*, below which was a path, then lawn and flower beds. All was enclosed by a laurel hedge. Alicia's special garden was where she planted *Magnolia conspicua*, *Fabiana imbricata*, Yuccas, Crinums, *Pernettya*, *Citrus* (now *Poncirus*) *trifoliata*, *Iris stylosa* (now *Iris unguicularis*), *Cistus* and other sun-lovers. They reflected her interest in tender plants. A few years later she designed a more formal area with clipped yews 'to connect my plot with the rest of the garden'.[6] It is known that Ellen Willmott helped her with suggestions (for example, to plant *Primula japonica* by the streamside) and with sources for plants, such as M. Tissot for roses, Gauntlett of Green Lane Nurseries, Redruth, Wood of Woodwith and Kirstace of Leeds for *Cistus*.[7]

In August 1920 she wrote to Sir William Dyer's successor at Kew, Sir David Prain, giving a view of how Lytchett was after the war: 'Things are very overgrown here and the place has not recovered [from] the war. My father in law who is 86 is not able to see about things so a good deal is left to me & I have been ill again so can't do much.'[8] But after Lord Eustace's death, when Lytchett became her permanent home and she had regained health, Alicia presided over the creation of a magnificent garden containing many varieties of plant. In 1931 she was asked to contribute an article on it for the Royal Horticultural Society's *Journal*. From this we know that she removed Lord Eustace's laurel hedge and replaced it with yew, removed the *Rhododendron ponticum* and put up a red brick wall and balustrade, allowing for a south facing border below it. This was planted with salvias, especially *Salvia farinacea*, *Ceratostigma willmottianum* (named after her friend Ellen Willmott), *Agapanthus*, *Lilium regale* and *Lilium auratum*, larkspur and lupins, with the Californian *Ceanothus floribunda* 'Gloire de Versailles' and *C. x Burkwoodii* behind them.

The walls of the house provided a home for tender shrubs, such as *Magnolia grandiflora*, and climbers like *Bignonia grandiflora* with 'scarlet trumpets from the end of August until late October', *Begonia capreolata*, and *Holboellia latifolia* which 'raced in five years to the top of the house'. Roses on her brick walls included the tender *Rosa* 'Mermaid' and its parent, *Rosa bracteata* 'with its glossy evergreen foliage and constant blooms of very sweet-scented white flowers'. Climbers elsewhere in the garden included *Vitis coignetiae* which produced regular displays of orange-red autumn colour with its huge leaves. Although Alicia had great successes (she reported *Hydrangea paniculata* as growing 12½ ft high), what really interested her was rarity. Her skill and enthusiasm were directed to coaxing productivity from a soil of very poor quality, thus to 'establish the more rare or uncommon plants, as there is such a variety of aspect of hill and dale, and a kindly climate, that in a few years time there ought to be many successes worth recording'.[9]

Lytchett Heath also had a walled kitchen garden where the specialities were white Muscat grapes, white-fleshed peaches and persimmons. This was kept locked but on its east-facing wall was a fruit cage containing gooseberries and redcurrants.[10] This, the fountains in the rose garden and 'planting for summer effects, with antirrhinums, dahlias and calceolarias' must have reminded Alicia of her old home. Other tender plants included *Jasminum primulinum*, *Abutilon megapotanicum*, *Physianthus albens*, *Carpentaria californica*, *Feijoa sellowiana*, *Carmichaelia odorata*, *Escallonia iveyi*, *Solanum jasminoides*, *Fremontia* (now *Fremontodendron*) *californica*, *Dendromecon rigida* and *Billardiera longiflora*, many of them Californian or Australian natives. An exotic feature was the hardy Chusan Palm, *Trachycarpus fortunei* (introduced by Robert Fortune in 1848).

To the west of the terraced gardens, the woodland valley garden was cleared of much of its *Rhododendron ponticum*, and Himalayan and Tibetan rhododendrons were substituted. In this moist, sheltered space under oak cover, Alicia planted azaleas, hydrangeas and her beloved bamboos, continuing an interest in the 'green garden' started at Didlington. In the archives at Chelsea Physic Garden is the catalogue of John Nichol, nurseryman of Green Lane Nurseries, Redruth, Cornwall, who specialised in hardy bamboos and included 'new and very rare species'. Alicia records planting species *spathiflora, anceps, viridi-glaucescens, simonis, fastuosa* and *mitis*. She continued to receive many recommendations for nursery suppliers from Ellen Willmott. Other inhabitants of the woodland garden were *Gunnera manicata, Rodgersia podophylla*, the Royal fern *Osmunda regalis*, the sensitive fern *Onoclea* 'brought from Massachusetts' and Todeas 'from Gippsland, Australia', as well as primroses and bluebells in spring. The wood was troubled by rabbits and roe deer and had to be wire-fenced to protect choice herbaceous plants such as gentians, primulas, montbretias, irises, antholizas and hostas.

So the 1920s was a period of intense gardening for Alicia. It started with post-war recovery, some selective tree felling and continued liaison with Kew to help re-establish vegetation after heath fires, and progressed until she had a garden worthy of the best. In 1921 Alicia was also re-sorting her life after the Didlington sales. She wrote to Sir David Prain asking where to send negatives of an awful storm which had felled timber at Didlington in January 1895 'which have now (since my old home was sold) come back to me'. She sorted some for the Egyptian Exploration Fund.[11] In short, it was a time of recovery, as for Britain in general. It must have been a healing process. As she noted in the *RHS Journal* article:

> I write these notes as a practical gardener, as some of the happiest moments of my life have been spent in manual labour in a garden. There is, I know, much enjoyment for those who attend shows, give orders for plants and plan colour schemes, but to me there seems infinitely more pleasure to be had from flowers after pricking out the seedlings myself, or selecting the spot and actually having a hand in their planting.

11

Tutankhamun Comes Good for Howard Carter

On 4th November 1922, Howard Carter, excavating in the Valley of the Kings, found the entrance to a tomb and cabled to his patron, Lord Carnarvon: 'At last have made wonderful discovery in the valley. A magnificent tomb with seals intact. Recovered same for your arrival. Congratulations. Carter.' It was thirty years since Carter had first arrived in Egypt as a seventeen-year-old under the patronage of Lord Amherst, to be trained in archaeology by Flinders Petrie and collect for the Amhersts. Lord Amherst had died in 1909, so was there any link between the Amhersts and the discovery of Tutankhamun's tomb? The answer is a tenuous 'yes' and the link is a financial one. It is tangential to Alicia's story, yet linked to 'The Deluge' and also to Carter as an artist: his main contribution to her *History*.

Carter's career had excessive ups and downs. In 1904 he was appointed Chief Inspector of Antiquities at the age of 25, after years of working at Deir el-Bahri for the Egypt Exploration Fund. This was one of two posts based on a division of territorial responsibility, he being based at Luxor. It was an extraordinary achievement for a practical man with no academic qualifications and it provided him with a house and financial security. However, his success was short lived. On 8th January 1905 at Saqqara an 'incident' occurred which was to have huge diplomatic repercussions. Fifteen French visitors arrived at the excavations rowdy and drunk. With some difficulty they were persuaded to pay admission but then demanded their money back as there were no candles for them to inspect the excavation safely. A substantial scuffle ensued and Carter supported his guards in resisting their entry, which led to an enquiry and a French/British diplomatic row. Carter, known to be stubborn and not seeing he had done anything wrong, refused to apologise and was effectively demoted to the Lower Egypt Office of Antiquities at Tanta. On 21st October 1905 he resigned and remained effectively unemployed until 1909. During this period he again turned to selling his paintings, the talent which had originally brought him to Egypt. With so many wealthy tourists about this activity must have supported him adequately – but it was hardly a steady source of income. The Amhersts' 'Deluge' occurred at the same time and, like Alicia, he must have felt distinctly insecure.[1]

By 1909, however, Carter had found a new patron in Lord Carnarvon who had been visiting Egypt since the 1905–6 season, partly for his health (he had been involved in a car accident in 1901). This started a new 'up' in Carter's financial fortunes, with a salary paid during excavations at Thebes. During the 1914–18 war he was employed in Cairo working for the Intelligence Department of the War Office, but he also continued painting, and possibly dealing in antiquities in the absence of his patron.

In 1915 his dealings returned to the Amhersts and, with Lord Carnarvon's help, he arranged for the sale of the 'Seven Sisters', the seven granite Sekhmet statues (which had probably been moved to Foulden before the Didlington sale of 1910) to the Metropolitan Museum of Art in New York (where they remain). He appears to have done this as a friend, without commission, and it would certainly have helped the Amhersts' finances at the time, though not his own. However, it led to other things, specifically a recommendation by Henry Kent, the Met's Secretary, as a potential agent for the Cleveland Museum of Art, then wishing to build up its Egyptian collection. From 1917 Carter acquired 15 per cent commission on all purchases he made for them.

The sale of the Sekhmets had been effected by Alicia's eldest sister, May, Lady William Cecil. The rest of the Amherst Egyptological collections and some books had been put into storage in Norwich where the Amhersts' ill fortune seemed to follow them. On 21st September 1912 May wrote to Newberry from Lou Casteou at Valescure, 'The things from Didlington, that were stored in Norwich, were unfortunately in the awful floods, and though a great deal, mercifully was untouched a great many books & treasures were terribly wet & among them objects from the museum, though luckily mostly stones, which are beginning to dry.'

She added, 'I am anxious to know if all the papyri are safe.'[2] Newberry knew the papyri intimately as he had published a catalogue *The Amherst Papyri* in 1899.

In 1919 Carter again acted for the Met in acquiring from the Norwich store a statue of Nebwau and Tenethat.[3] Then the Dowager Lady Amherst died and it may have been that, freed from their mother's devotion to the collection, her eldest daughter and her husband decided to sell the whole collection.[4] Carter was the obvious man to produce a catalogue as he had, in large part, been responsible for building up the collection and had also been acting as an adviser for Sotheby's, the auctioneers. In 1920–1 Carter allowed the Cleveland Museum to see the catalogue[5] and at the Amherst sale of 13–17th June 1921, £14,533 was raised, some of the artefacts being acquired for Cleveland by Carter on the agreed 15 per cent commission.

The importance of this to the subsequent discovery of Tutankhamun's tomb lies in the fact that Carter made certain undertakings to Lord Carnarvon which were only possible because he had an independent income.

About the time that Alicia was moving to become permanently resident at Lytchett Heath in 1922, Carter was at Highclere Castle to discuss with his patron the future of their excavations. They had had limited success in the Valley of the Kings and Carnarvon wanted to give up. Carter, however, wanted 'just one more season', particularly to investigate an area covered with debris and old huts near the tomb of Rameses VI. According to Carter's biographer, T.G.H. James, this had been left alone because it was too near the tomb to be excavated during the busy tourist season. The meeting is recorded second-hand by the author Charles Breasted and based on what Carter told him;[6] it included naming the search for Tutankhamun and *an offer by Carter to finance a further season's digging himself*. This is in accord with further offers he made, for which there is direct evidence in a letter from Carter to Newberry dated 18th January 1930:

> Almina, the Countess of Carnarvon, for whom I have been carrying out the work, having completed her part of the undertaking naturally did not renew her concession which terminated on 31st October last. Last April I offered to complete the technical work that still remains to be done in the laboratory at my cost, and further to help the Antiquity Department in the

very intricate undertaking of removing those large shrines from the tomb of Tutankhamun.[7]

Carter's offer apparently convinced Carnarvon to continue financing one more season. It was a bet which paid off. Carter took only four days to find the tomb, from 1st to 4th November 1922. On 26th November he replied to Carnarvon's query, 'Can you see anything?', 'Yes, wonderful things.'

The financing of Egyptian excavations, and the cultural sensitivities of Egypt in a time of increasing nationalism are important to this story. The Antiquities Department, dominated by French and British officials, lacked the resources to excavate and conserve the country's heritage. It was only because of wealthy foreign investors, like the Amhersts and Carnarvons, that excavations took place at all, but it was a sensitive area. Gradually, as the twentieth century developed, the Egyptian government assumed more responsibility and developed a greater sense of how they could enforce cultural ownership. But this took time. Even in 1930, eight years after the discovery of Tutankhamun, Carter was writing to Newberry, 'I should also like to point out to you that neither the tomb of Tutankhamun nor the laboratory have been officially taken over from us by the Eg. Gov. ... Yet the Eg. Gov. makes full use of them without having attempted to take them over nor render to us any recompense for the same.'[8] Carter often walked a tightrope in his dealings in cultural artefacts and in getting permissions and excavation concessions. Eventually, in 1930, Lady Carnarvon was recompensed by the Egyptian government for her husband's investment in the concession to the tune of £35,867 13s 8d, 25 per cent of which was promised to Carter as their principal excavator. He eventually received £8,558 2s 9d.[9] In turn, the objects were dutifully extracted and conserved by Carter over a ten year period and given to the Cairo Museum where they remain.

Yet it was only the fact that Howard Carter was in a position to offer to finance 'just one more season' that persuaded Lord Carnarvon to renew his licence and find the tomb. Carter could afford to make the offer because he had private resources, partly accrued from commission on sales of antiquities, including those of the Amhersts; he always acknowledged his debt to Lord Amherst (see pages 20–1).

Above: The changing rooms at
the Italianate bathing pool of
the original Didlington Hall,
Norfolk. Very little remains of
Alicia's childhood home – it
was demolished in the 1950s.
Courtesy of Elizabeth Orr Sutcliffe.

Left: Cecil John Rhodes by George
Frederic Watts. Alicia knew
Cecil's brother Frankie and family
connections eased her reception
at Cape Town during the visit
with her new husband in 1899-
1900. The visit made them ardent
supporters of British colonialism.
*Copyright: National Portrait
Gallery, London.*

Left: Viscount Alfred Milner by Hugh de Twenebrokes Glazebrook. Alicia, along with Gertrude Bell, worked to populate the Transvaal with British female emigrants in support of Milner's colonial policies. Some of these started farms and market gardens. During the Great War the Milner Committee noted that two-thirds of Britain's food was imported from outside the British Empire and thus thought insecure. *Copyright: National Portrait Gallery, London.*

Below: Joseph ('Joe') Chamberlain (left) with Arthur James Balfour, 1st Earl of Balfour by Sydney Prior. Alicia and Evelyn supported Chamberlain's approach to colonial expansion and to Tariff Reform which would have supported British trade with the colonies – an alternative model to today's European Union and now long abandoned. *Copyright: National Portrait Gallery, London.*

Left: Alicia painted watercolours from an early age, especially on her travels. Gardens were a favourite subject; this is of La Mortola on the French/Italian border.
Courtesy of Lord Rockley.

Left: Alicia's watercolour of the view from a villa in Nice, November 1929.
Courtesy of Lord Rockley.

Left: Sir William Matthew Flinders Petrie by George Frederic Watts. Flinders Petrie was the Egyptologist Lord Amherst used to train Howard Carter in excavation skills – and augment his collection of antiquities.
Copyright: National Portrait Gallery, London.

Left: Gertrude Jekyll by Sir William Newzam Prior Nicholson. Gertrude Jekyll, then primarily a gardening journalist, reviewed Alicia's *A History of Gardening in England.* There is no evidence they ever met, though they had a friend in common – Ellen Willmott.
Copyright: National Portrait Gallery, London.

Left: Alicia's copy (made in 1920) from her sketch of Et-nub-El Hamman on the right bank of the Nile, made in January 1895 during her first visit to Egypt. *In private collection.*

Below: Alicia's watercolour of a 'Village near Elephant's bath, Katugastota January 9th 1927'. She always observed local life closely. *In private collection.*

Above: A watercolour of the Inner Temple Garden by Lady Victoria Manners,
a plate from Alicia's *London Parks and Gardens* (1907).
Below: A watercolour of Chelsea Physic Garden by Lady Victoria Manners showing the
statue of Sir Hans Sloane, a plate from Alicia's *London Parks and Gardens* (1907).

Left: The entrance to Lou Casteou, the Amhersts' three-story Italianate villa on the Côte d'Azur on rising ground behind San Raphael.

Below: Lou Casteou-the frontage facing towards the sea. Building started in 1903 and it was three years later that news of financial ruin reached the family while staying here.

Above: Alicia's watercolour
of her home in adulthood
- Lytchett Heath - after
she had extensively
remodelled the terraces
to provide microclimates
for tender plants.
In private collection.

Below: Alicia's watercolour
of the view to the sea
from the library at Lytchett
Heath. April 1929.
Courtesy of Lord Rockley.

Left: A portrait in oils of Alicia by her talented daughter Maud. She wears the Maltese Cross as a Dame of Justice of the Order of St John of Jerusalem and holds a stem of the yellow form of the Gloriosa lily she had collected on her visit to South Africa in 1899-1900. *In private collection.*

Left: Alicia's husband Evelyn, First Baron Rockley of Lytchett Heath by his daughter Maud. *In private collection.*

Above: Oriel, daughter of
Maud, Alicia's youngest
offspring. Painted by
her mother, Maud.
In private collection.

Left: 'Among the Firs of
British Columbia', Alicia's
watercolour from *Wild
Flowers of the Great Dominions
of the British Empire.*

Left: 'Canadian Summer Flowers and Berries', Alicia's watercolour from *Wild Flowers*. Includes *Lilium canadense* (top left), *Aquilegia canadense* and *Solidago* (top right), *Rosa setigera* (bottom right) and, her favourite, Indian Paintbrush *(Castilleja miniata)* (centre).

Left: 'Some Australian Wild Flowers', Alicia's watercolour from *Wild Flowers*. Includes *Telopea speciosissima* (centre), *Grevillea robusta* (right), *Blandfordia flammea* (right below Grevillea).

Left: 'Western Australia in Spring'. Alicia's watercolour from *Wild Flowers* painted near Margaret River, October 1926, showing Red Gum (left) and Jarrah trees (right), spiky Grass trees festooned with Coral creeper and Kangaroo paws (bottom left). The blues are *Hovea, Leschenaultia, Dampiera* and Swan River daisies.

Left: 'Spring Flowers of Western Australia'. Alicia's watercolour from *Wild Flowers* including *Anigozanthus manglesii* (top left), *Patersonia occidentalis* (top right), *Kennedya prostrata* (bottom right). The blues are *Leschenaultia biloba* (left), *Hovea elliptica* (right) and *Brachycome iberidifolia* (bottom).

Left: 'Flowers of the Australian Salt-bush Plains and Desert'. Alicia's watercolour from *Wild Flowers* including *Grevillea eriostachya* (top right), *Hibiscus hugelii* (centre left) and *Clianthus dampieri* (centre right).

Left: 'Flowering Trees of New Zealand'. Alicia's watercolour from *Wild Flowers* showing *Corynocarpus laevigatus* fruits (top left), *Olearia semidentata* (top right), *Fuchsia excorticata* (bottom right) and *Corokia cotoneaster* (bottom left).

Left: 'A New Zealand Forest Sketch'. Alicia's watercolour from *Wild Flowers,* painted near Wellington, showing *Laurelia Novae-Zelandiae* and tree ferns *Cyathea medularis* (back) with *Cyathea dealbata* and *Dicksonia squarrosa.*

Left: 'Some African Flowers'. Alicia's watercolour from *Wild Flowers* shows *Protea abyssinica* (top right), *Erythrina caffra* (red, top left) and *Sandersonia aurantiaca* (orange bells, bottom right). The blue flowers are *Asystasia* (top left), *Clerodendron myricoides* (centre), *Lapeyrousia rhodesiana* (centre bottom) and *Aptosimum lineare* (bottom left).

Above: Lytchett Heath today.
Courtesy of Lord Rockley.

Below: St Aldhelm's Chapel, built at Lytchett Heath in 1897 and in the curtilage of which Alicia and Evelyn are buried.
Courtesy of Lord Rockley.

Left: Evelyn and Alicia's gravestone bearing a Maltese Cross – the different sections of which relate to the noble families of Europe. *Courtesy of Lord Rockley.*

Left: A plaque to Evelyn and Alicia (unfortunately fire-damaged) within St Aldhelm's Chapel, which mentions her links to the Worshipful Company of Gardeners and to the Order of St John of Jerusalem. *Courtesy of Lord Rockley.*

The discovery of the tomb of Tutankhamun caused a sensation in Britain (largely orchestrated by Lord Carnarvon's shrewd exclusive deal with *The Times* newspaper). It inspired yet another bout of popular mania for all things Egyptian.[10] It is not clear how the Amhersts took this turn of events nor how they viewed the Exhibition of Decorative Arts in Paris in 1925, which launched the Egyptian-inspired Art Deco look. Perhaps it was as much a matter of regret as, for Alicia, was the loss of her old home. Her life had moved apart from Carter's, and also from that of Percy Newberry, who, from 1929 to 1933, had been Professor of Ancient Egyptian History and Archaeology at Cairo. On 9th January 1933 she wrote rather formally to 'Professor Newberry' from aboard the ship *Ausonia* from Venice, inviting him to meet her at the Heliopolis Palace hotel in Cairo where she was to stay with Evelyn during the International Railway Congress. They were to go on to Jerusalem on 11th because Evelyn, though Secretary of the Order of St John of Jerusalem all through the Great War, had never had a chance to visit the city. They would then return to Cairo for the Congress from 17th to 31st. She said how much she wanted to see him, 'although it is so many years since we met'.[11]

Newberry outlived Alicia by eight years. Carter died in London of Hodgkin's disease on 2nd March 1939 but Alicia, by then severely ill herself, did not attend his funeral.

12

Colonial Travel

Alicia's work for the South African Colonization Society from 1901 was reduced after the First World War as the number of emigrants declined. The structure of emigration was changing and organisations changed to accommodate it. In 1917 a Joint Council of Emigration Societies was formed under Alicia's chairmanship, and, after the war, in December 1919, this joined with the South African Colonization Society to form the Society for Overseas Settlement of British Women (SOSBW). Essentially, this existed to assist women trained for jobs vacated by men going to the trenches who were subsequently left in financial difficulties when these men returned to resume their peace-time occupations. Alicia was Vice-Chairman (always with one other) from 1921 until she became ill in 1938.

She was involved from the beginning in financial negotiations with the Treasury. In June 1917 she gave evidence on behalf of the Joint Council to the new 'Empire Committee', appointed by the government under Lord Tennyson. It met at Spencer House. When SOSBW was founded she called a joint meeting of the finance committees on 30th April 1919 to estimate that £5,000 p.a. would be needed for their work – and this became the settlement from the Treasury until 1931 when it was cut back to £3,300. SOSBW's role was to advise on government policy for emigration (which, in the 1920s, was increasing to Canada and Australia), to assess individuals, and families with children, for their suitability and to oversee their travel, safety and employment once abroad.

In 1925 Evelyn was short-listed for the Governor-Generalship of Australia, owing to his own long history of supporting the Empire and colonisation – interests completely in accord with Alicia's. It was not to be, however. There were other sources of sadness. In June 1926, Alicia's sister Sybil died while staying with Florence at 6, William Street in London. She was buried on 26th at St Michael and All Saints, Didlington, the family church. Nevertheless, Evelyn and Alicia did go abroad that year, first to Canada, then on to Australia and New Zealand as part of an empire parliamentary delegation. Alicia was thus enabled to continue her work on behalf of the Society for the Overseas Settlement of British Women and the Victoria League. It was also a great opportunity to enjoy the botanical riches of these countries, particularly the antipodean territories which she had not visited before. Dr Arthur Hill, the third Director of the Royal Botanic Gardens, Kew to be on friendly terms with her, sent letters of introduction. Alicia noted on 24th July 1926 that the visit would be 'hurried' but 'still I shall have a fair time in Western Australia which will be the most wonderful of all.'[1]

They went first to Canada and Newfoundland and it is clear from her later writings[2] that she had become interested in what we would now call ecology and ethnobotany. She understood the difference between native and naturalised plants (i.e. those which had evolved *in situ* and those introduced and 'gone wild'), known introductions from abroad of horticultural value and those plants of aggressive, colonising tendency called 'invasives' like *Opuntia* and Viper's Bugloss. In Canada she showed interest in how maple syrup was produced, observed the Native American use of bark from *Betula papyrifera* and noted the economic value of the resins from the native conifers. She wrote about spring and summer flowers, the specific flora of the prairies, with a particular note on the genus *Castilleja*: 'No one who has seen the Indian paintbrushes can fail to associate them with their memories of Canada.'[3]

Her trip to New Zealand included visits to both Wellington and Christchurch where she was interviewed and reported in the press. She used Dr Hill's introductions to botanical experts and she wrote back to him from a 'rolling' RMS *Tahiti* on 30th September 1926:

Dr Cockayne welcomed my visit as it strengthened his hand in trying to stop the introduction of heather into the National Parks[4] [she had plenty of experience of heather from Lytchett] ... There is a wonderful piece of real primeval Beech near, some 16 miles, Wellington Wainuiomata we were taken to, & also within the city a place Willows Bush where Dr Cockayne & Mr Mackenzie are planning a real collection of N.Z. plants – for alpines, ferns etc as well as the native Wellington beech – an out of doors museum of NZ plants. The place is well united [suited?] to it and is quite near the city within its precincts. The Mayor is supporting it & I think my enthusiasm has helped over the project.[5]

She obviously made an impression on New Zealanders: a violet-blue hebe was named 'Alicia Amherst' in her honour.

Alicia's summary of the flora of New Zealand will be instantly understood by today's botanical travellers: the links in genera between New Zealand and South America (she cites *Nothofagus* and *Laurelia*), the whiteness of flowers, the common nature of juvenile forms of growth on trees and shrubs, natural hybrids and the highly localised distribution of species. She also showed an advanced understanding of conservation issues, especially the destructiveness of introduced animals such as wild pigs and deer, and the importance of National Parks, particularly in view of the depletion of the Kauri forest. She noted that 576 species of 320 genera from 78 families were 'alien intruders' in the native vegetation but that they were out-competed everywhere except in burnt and cultivated areas. Just as she had listened to local botanists, she also made ethnographic observations:

> The Maoris use the fronds of *Cyathea dealbata*, the Silver Tree-fern or Ponga to spread on the floors of their huts for bedding, laying them silver side down, so that the dust from the spores should not blow about but they use them silver side up to mark a path through the bush, as the white can be clearly seen in the dark, perhaps from some slight phosphorescence as well as from their silver hue.[6]

The record she made of her visit to Tasmania gives us a good idea of how she travelled as a field botanist:

> The safest place for the traveller to study the wonders of the bush at the present time would be in the Natal Park, a reserve of 35,500 acres situated fifty miles from Hobart, up the valley of the Derwent, with its orchards and hop-gardens. The railway runs to the entrance near the Russell Falls, where the river descends 120 feet among tall Swamp Gums and masses of Tree-ferns which overhang it. Six miles further within the area near Lake Fenton, about 3,000 feet above the sea, there are huts for tourists, and tracks from there radiate through the bush. Some are wide, others are merely marked by upright stakes to serve as guides. One of these leads for seven miles to the

summit of Mount Field, 7,721 feet. Thus many of the typical plants of Tasmania from the lowland up to the alpine can be observed without the danger of being 'bushed', and with no worse accident befalling than by being tripped up by Tanglefoot.[7]

She had a fine appreciation of the structure of the vegetation and how some plant types take the ecological place of similar plants in other countries. 'Some of the Tasmanian Richeas are almost Screw Pines. They take the place of the Cabbage trees of New Zealand or the Grass trees of West Australia and are in fact often called Grass trees in Tasmania.'[8] As always, she noted what could be horticulturally useful back home:

> There is still a wonderful native flora which, though hardly sufficiently valued by the early settlers in their desire to reproduce homeland surroundings, is greatly appreciated today. Gardeners in Great Britain are reversing the picture, and with some success are trying to cultivate all the showy plants they can collect from Tasmania, which has a climate in many respects similar to the warmer parts of the British Isles.[9]

Her writings about Australia show a sophisticated botanical understanding of its flora, and particularly of the geological theory of Gondwanaland and Continental Drift, with its explanation for the existence of common families of plants in countries of the southern hemisphere now geographically isolated from one another. She had read the journals of the botanist and plant hunter Allan Cunningham who had been responsible for introducing many Australian plants into cultivation in England earlier in the century[10] and was also aware that 46 species of Australian plants had come to Britain as seed in sheep's wool.[11] She understood the importance of fire in Australian ecology and noted the problem of invasive plants like blackberry, *Inula graveolens*, *Cynara carduncellus*, Water Hyacinth (*Eichornia crassipes*), Evening Primrose (*Oenothera biennis*) and Purple Foxglove (*Digitalis purpurea*), as well as 'biological control' agents, such as *Cactoblastis cactorum* being used against *Opuntia* moth. Of *Xanthium spinosum* she noted that it had 'arrived in the tails of horses from Valparaiso.'[12]

Her Australian visit took her to Queensland, where she noted thirty species in one day[13] and New South Wales where she observed the clearance of land for farming and settlement and the seasonality of rain:

'There seems to be nothing but dry sticks and sand in the creek where the kangaroos have been scratching for water ... the moment the rain descends New South Wales once more looks like a large park in which a landscape gardener had planted a great variety of choice and rare shrubs and had scattered the seed of Golden and White Everlastings to finish the picture.'[14]

In the State of Victoria she noted the rare *Humea* (now *Calomeria* *elegans*, the Incense Plant, which was regularly bedded out in summer in Victorian England, with its leaves and flowers smelling of tobacco. She travelled with Evelyn by train: 'The Grampians have been described as one of Nature's Wonderlands, and there within a small area of pretty scenery a beautiful collection of some of the most charming flowers can be enjoyed in the summer. They are easy of access to those accustomed to Australian trains, who are undaunted by the effort to leave the Adelaide–Melbourne express at about four in the morning.'[15] She used the 'luxurious Trans-Australian railway' to cover the 1,000 mile journey from Port Augusta in South Australia across the Nullarbor ('no tree') plain to Kalgoorlie in Western Australia. She remarked on the plains of grass and saltbush which she clearly found attractive, described the famous Sturt's Desert Pea[16] and observed certain Aboriginal practices. Of Pitury (*Duboisia hopwoodii*) she noted that they 'chew it as the Peruvians do coca. They sit together passing it round or sometimes smoking the dry leaves. It is said to be a powerful stimulant, assuaging hunger and enabling long journeys to be taken with little food. Unfortunately this Pitury of the natives only produces headaches in Europeans.'[17]

In Western Australia she was aware of the extent of the indigenous flora resulting from the isolation of the region: 'There are plants with pedigrees stretching into geological periods which have survived in this corner of the globe, cut off by sea and desert from outside influences', but was also aware that it was threatened by the spread of agriculture 'during the last fifty years'.[18] She painted a vivid picture of the seasonal flowering, the Black Boys and Kangaroo Paws and special groups such as sundews, orchids and the blue drifts of *Hovea heterophylla*.[19]

In the Northern Territory she described botanising 'near the railway inland from Darwin' and finding a carpeting plant with pale mauve-grey flowers which she sent to Kew with the provisional identification of *Dentella linearis*. Five years later she obtained a fresh specimen through friends in Darwin and Kew named it, to her delight, a new species: *Dentella dioeca.*[20] Altogether, Alicia was entranced by Australia and succeeded in visiting every part: 'These botanical researches, although full of interest, give no idea of the stretch of delicate grey and vivid green on which the writer had stood, while the black cockatoos screamed overhead, and the sun blazed down on the Gum trees which formed a background to the still water where the emus came down to drink.'[21] She gave reports of the deserts flowering because of strongly erratic rainfall and her lasting impression was one of contrasts: 'Two pictures of Australia remain vivid – one of pale sun-baked ground that once was grass and dull grey-green trees, the other a brighter scene of waving grass and golden flowers bathed in smiling sunshine.'[22]

The botanical interlude by railway, made possible by Evelyn's parliamentary interests and her charitable ones, made a deep impression on Alicia and, in the last decade of her life, partly inspired her book *Wild Flowers of the Great Dominions of the British Empire* (1935). It was intended to serve the traveller or settler but turned out to be one of the best summaries of the flora of these countries – and the threats to their conservation – to have been written.

13

A Literary Reprise in the 1930s

Alicia had been much involved in charitable work in the 1920s, for the Chelsea Physic Garden and for the Society for Overseas Settlement of British Women, among other causes. Her husband Evelyn, meanwhile, continued his busy parliamentary career. His concerns were as diverse as the telephone service, young offenders, the honours system and press coverage of divorce, as well as railways and the mines, although both of them had interests in empire settlement. In 1929 Evelyn decided not to stand again for election to Birmingham (Aston) but in 1930 was appointed chairman of a Board of Trade Committee to examine miners' deaths from coal gas. In 1934 he was given a peerage and named Baron Rockley of Lytchett Heath in the New Year honours; he continued his work on mines, chairing a Royal Commission and delivering the Rockley Report on Safety in Coal Mines (1938).

Alicia, meanwhile, as Lady Rockley, found the 1930s an occasion for a literary reprise with two new works. The first, grandly titled, *Wild Flowers of the Great Dominions of the British Empire* started life as a smaller work on the wild flowers of Canada alone, but was later expanded to cover all the areas to which she and Evelyn had travelled. It was published by Macmillan in 1935 and dealt with Canada, Australia, New Zealand and South Africa with a 'cursory glance' at Rhodesia and Kenya, but omitted India and the West Indies, of which she had no direct knowledge. The idea had been long in gestation – indeed it dated from 1926 when in Auckland she had found her room decorated with native flowers with unfamiliar local names and resolved to fill the need for a handy guide.

This work brought together all Alicia's botanical interests and her passion for travel. It was a confident book, illustrated for the first time mostly with her own watercolours rather than illustrations by others. It revealed a happy marriage, being dedicated to her husband 'without whose unfailing encouragement this book would never have been written, or the sketches made with which it is illustrated'.

A reviewer[1] noted that her real love was Australia – the subject of her grand trip in 1926. Nevertheless, the book collects her experiences gathered over three decades of travel and it is illuminating to see how she covers her earlier African journeys in South Africa, Rhodesia and Kenya. Alicia always wrote in an all-encompassing way, with an ability to hold the overview already apparent in her earliest work on the *History*. For example, she compared the flora of Africa and Australia in the broadest terms: which botanical families predominated and which formed their ecological equivalents in each country;[2] the effects of wind and rain and how the studies of botany and ecology had developed.[3] She was very conscious of conservation efforts and noted the need for reserves and the balance required to provide timber.[4]

The Cape was obviously a delight to her: '... it gives a thrill for the first time to gather a bunch of Arum Lilies by the roadside to those accustomed to seeing them priced at a shilling each in Covent Garden market'. She called the heaths 'one of the glories of South Africa'.[5] She visited Table Mountain by rail, enjoyed *Rochea coccinea* and noted, 'almost every gardener has heard of the Disas of Table Mountain', adding that these terrestrial orchids, unlike the arum lilies 'are carefully protected and picking them is a punishable offence. But any such laws are difficult to enforce, and just as in England whole districts have been denuded of common flowers, such as Primroses or Foxgloves, the Cape Peninsula with its wondrous wealth of flowers is not what it used to be.'[6]

She observed how the spurges (euphorbias) 'in general effect resemble the Cacti of the New World, but do not have their lovely flowers'[7] and the enormous effect of locusts: 'They shadow the earth and as they pass there is green veld in front of them and brown veld behind: and not a leaf, not a flower or blade of grass is left, nothing but earth and stones.'[8]

On Alicia's original trip to South Africa soon after her marriage, she was entranced by the bulbous flora. In the review she notes how many of the bulbs are actually poisonous to humans and cattle.[9] Of *Gladiolus*, *Freesia*, *Watsonia*, *Babiana*, *Aristea* and *Ixia*, she commended particularly the green-flowered *Ixia viridiflora*: 'No wonder it has been found necessary to protect this unique flower from ruthless gatherers.'[10] Of the Bush lilies (*Clivia miniata*) she noted '… to enjoy a number of them growing together in a kloof it is necessary to brave ticks and such-like insects and perhaps snakes.'[11] Of the species which form seed tumbleweeds which blow across the veld (*Brunsvigia, Haemanthus* and *Boophane*), they '… can afford quite an amusing chase on a fast Basuto pony.'[12] Knowing she was a good horsewoman, one wonders whether this was an observation or a memory.

This mix of botanical knowledge and ecological understanding is pitched at a comfortable level for the general tourist: 'Flaming red is such a characteristic of Africa's flora that no doubt the reader has noticed how red prevails in almost every type of flowering plant, just as white is outstanding in New Zealand and yellow most prominent in Australia.'[13]

She also described a journey from Cape Town to Pretoria through the Hex River Valley beyond Worcester where 'the vegetation changes, getting more and more Karroid'.[14] The Karroo deserts support succulents such as *Testudinaria, Elephantipes, Stapelia, Hoodia, Sarcocaulon* and succulent pelagoniums and *Harpagophytum* (under the name 'Devil's Claw' now a popular herbal remedy for rheumatism in Europe). She saw all these, plus *Haworthia, Fenestraria, Gasteria*, succulent cucurbits (plants of the genus Cucurbitaceae) with their deep roots and the ancient two-leaved *Welwitschia* – 'These sun-baked lands do indeed hide some weird freaks of nature.'

Of Natal she commented on the orchids and squills, noted that the (now popular) genus *Dierama*, commonly known as Angel's Fishing Rod, seemed to vary in colour, 'being pink near the sea and more purple inland' whereas *Zantedeschia rehmannii* is 'a far prettier pink in its natural habitat than when removed to gardens or greenhouses.'[15] The Drakensberg Mountains she seemed to love, being particularly taken by the beauty of *Greyia sutherlandii*.[16]

To end the book, she covered, briefly, the flora of Rhodesia and Kenya. Rhodesia she had first visited in November and December 1899 – the honeymoon trip which had been so productive of new botanical species, some named after her. Almost forty years later, one she particularly celebrated was *Kaempferia cecilae*, a relative of the culinary ginger and 'a plant akin to Orchids [which] rises out of the damp ground, with pale purple blooms almost as luscious as a hot-house *Cattleya*.'[17]

Of the Kenyan flora she rarely mentions a plant without noting an associated ethnobotanical use:

> Another small deciduous tree (*Clausena anisata*) has heads of white flowers and very aromatic twigs and leaves. The fragrant twigs are used by the Masai for cleaning their teeth ... A larger tree is most formidably armed with spiky excrescences (*Zanthoxylum*), and the stem, twigs and scented leaves are all covered with large prickles. Although so fierce-looking the timber is like satinwood and the bark is used by natives as a cough mixture.[18]

She was aware of the problems of over-grazing, and over-population, and the effects of slash and burn agriculture, as well as early efforts to repair this by societies such as Men of the Trees and the African Forest Scouts.[19] On Mount Kilimanjaro, she was amazed by the 'Tree Groundsels' which are such a surprising feature to travellers: 'They seem like Druidical monoliths ... They have giant heads of flowers in proportion to their massive bodies, which are just like the Groundsel given to canaries but on a Brobdingnagian scale.' *Lobelia giberroa* she noted as growing 25 to 30 foot tall.

In her postscript, Alicia showed how aware she had become of the huge changes in transport that had taken place over her lifetime:

> Travelling is now so rapid, and people who forty years ago slowly made their way by bullock wagon, or more probably walked with native carriers, now dash over excellent roads in high-powered cars after traversing hundreds of miles by rail. They can vary their mode of progression by employing the luxurious boats on the Nile or they may even arrive at their destination faster still by air.

The book received good reviews from botanists. Writing in the *Journal of Botany* for September 1935 'A.B.R.' commented that it fulfilled a need 'from folks proposing to visit one or other of the overseas Dominions ... for a book on the wild plants of the country, less cumbersome and erudite than a strictly botanical "Flora"' – which was precisely its aim. He called it 'charming' and 'free from the misspellings of plant-names which not infrequently mar semi-popular works'. This was because Alicia had been thorough, staff at Kew had assisted with the work and William Hales at Chelsea Physic Garden had proof-read it. However, the reviewer was less keen on the poetry – which Alicia had always incorporated into her writings, however scholarly – 'Lady Rockley follows the custom of some of the early Victorian botanists who "enriched" their text with quotations from the poets – good, bad and indifferent.'

A reviewer in the *Kew Bulletin* particularly praised her watercolours: '"Among the Firs of British Columbia" is a fine example of the author's skill as an artist ... Possibly the most interesting of Lady Rockley's series of flower studies is her plate of the remarkable West Australian orchids of the genus *Caladenia*, and many will consider the sketch of "The Old White Gum" the best picture in the book.'[21] The reviewer went on:

> When one knows the rapidity with which she travelled and the vast distances she covered, often making her sketches from train or car, Lady Rockley is to be congratulated on having presented to plant lovers both at home and overseas so arresting a picture of the botanical wonders of the British Dominions. By her book she deserves to be styled not only a citizen and gardener of London but also of the British Dominions.

That last comment must have given her great pleasure, referring as it did, to the reception of *A History of Gardening in England* in 1895. There were other similarities between the two publications. Just as the *History* had a stupendous bibliography of primary source, so for *Wild Flowers* ... she listed seven pages of 'Some of the Books Consulted', including manuscripts of Sir Joseph Banks's visit to Newfoundland, floras and checklists, *Index Kewensis* and narratives of exploration, such as the journals of David Douglas. This was not merely a light book for tourists.

Alicia's last book was published in 1938 by *Country Life*, and in New York by Charles Scribner's Sons. It was called *Historic Gardens of England*. Its purpose was two-fold. Firstly, the 68-page summary of gardening in England was intended to update her *History* to fill in developments in the years 1895 to 1938. Secondly, it provided a thumbnail sketch of her own selection of 96 of the finest gardens of England, each with a picture provided from the archive of *Country Life*. She dedicated it to her son, Robert, 'who shares with me a keen interest in plants and a love of gardening'.

The book is interesting because Alicia allowed herself to be more opinionated than in the *History*. For example, she was far more damning of the destructiveness to the formal tradition that had been the legacy of Lancelot Brown and Humphrey Repton:

> The landscape school of gardeners achieved some remarkable successes and created some beautiful scenes, but at great cost, as in most cases they destroyed before they planted, and their work of destruction was at one time so formidable that it is a wonder that any garden of the old formal pattern survived.[22]

Her own opinions and preferences showed through, if subtly:

> They were unimpressed by the charm of a long vista of chequered light and shade, and were not stirred by the spirit of stately trunks towering towards the sky like the columns of a great cathedral … They saw no beauty in a well-kept Yew hedge as a dark background to glowing flowers … Flowers were quite out of the reckoning. The garden was to be landscape so contrived that it should inspire certain feeling …[23]

She was more censorious of the usurpation of interest in herbaceous borders by the popularity of bedding and half-hardy plants, commenting that 'the regrettable side to this form of gardening was the neglect of hardier plants.'[24] She condemned the excesses of Victorian rockeries, but was approving when the point was to grow alpine collections …[25]

In the chapter 'Gardens of Today' she ascribed interest in gardening to the huge influx of new plants from plant collectors and its boost to the nursery trade. She noted the increase in the number of gardening newspapers and books and in RHS membership, from 4,750 in 1900 to over 35,000 in 1938. Huge numbers were turning up at shows, and specialised societies for certain classes of plants were springing up. One of her most interesting comments, given her aristocratic background, is that on the classlessness of gardening:

> The visitor represents all classes, from the King and Queen to the possessor of a minute back garden who has to save up the half-crown for entrance on the last day [of the Chelsea show].
>
> It is one of the most interesting features of this great revival that it has spread through every rank in life. The slum dweller does his best to brighten up the streets with window boxes, and there are not wanting societies to assist him in this laudable ambition. The sweet old-fashioned cottage garden is still a joy in the few unspoilt country districts, and luckily the promiscuous and rapid spreading of cities into the countryside is somewhat mitigated by

the cheerful little gardens which surround the bungalows of every shape and size. Many a small suburban villa garden is a thing of beauty, and bears the mark of patient labour and skilful handling, and often no mean knowledge of plants.[26]

Her thumbnail sketches of gardens have an augmented interest because they contain as much about the architecture, history and family status of their owners as their gardens. In her long life she had visited widely and was concerned to comment from personal experience as well as put the garden in its historical context and note any later changes. She described the period of each garden and its structural features, and only occasionally gave additional horticultural detail. For example, of Loseley Park she noted without elaboration that 'Much of the modern planting was devised by Miss Gertrude Jekyll.'[27] Her opinions are not suppressed, however. Of Cobham Hall, Kent, she writes that the Earl of Darnley was 'an artist in garden colour' (Plate 72); Townhill Park, Hampshire (Plate 94) she considered the best site in the country for the cultivation of *Lilium* (now *Cardiocrinum*) *giganteum*; Burton Park, Sussex (Plate 96) she commended for its treatment of trained groundcover roses.

Perhaps the real interest of her final book is that it provides a snapshot of the greatest gardens of 1938 and the superb *Country Life* photography must have pleased her as a practical photographer herself. Since *Country Life* was started only in 1897, these pictures were not a resource available to her when she wrote the *History*. Many of the gardens featured no longer exist and one suspects that a similar exercise today would provide a similar snapshot, equally likely to be out of date in under a century. Gardens are ephemeral creations but perhaps that was, and is, their charm.

Evelyn retired from the House of Lords after a final speech on pithead baths in March 1939. It was a time of ill health for both him and Alicia who had a serious operation in 1938, probably for breast cancer. There is an extraordinary paragraph in Alicia's *Odd Notes* (made for her children in the summer of 1941) and transcribed from dictation when she was dying. It refers to the famous physicist Lord Kelvin, who was friendly with Alicia and Evelyn and interested in new technological development such as incandescent light: 'It was at Lord Kelvin's house that I saw the Radium that Madame Curie had given him. He took it out of his pocket in a little tube and I had it in my hand, a shining light for a moment and Lord Kelvin said: "This is the nearest thing to magic I know of."' Becquerel had discovered radium in 1896. Between then and Lord Kelvin's death in 1907, neither he, nor Alicia, could have known of the extraordinary danger of the radiation to which they were exposing themselves. Alicia's following comment – 'How little did I think I would know so much about radium before the end of my journey.' – strongly implies that she had radiation treatment for her cancer. We know from her grand-daughter, Oriel Robinson, she found this hard and recommended to her family that if any of them developed the disease they should not bother to be treated.

At the outbreak of World War II Alicia was at Lytchett Heath. Her grandson Jock (son of her daughter Margaret) remembered her saying, 'How awful that such terrible things are happening on such a lovely day.' With the reformation of the Women's Land Army there must, for Alicia, have been a terrible sense of *déjà vu*. There were seven Amherst/Cecil grandchildren at Lytchett at this time and they were put on the top floor (with a fire escape) under the supervision of a Mrs Holbrook who cooked for them all. Downstairs was taken over by an Army Brigade as their HQ. The family built a trench to protect the grandchildren, but the real risk was fire from aircraft crashing, especially during the Battle of Britain. Dorset heathland was readily inflammable and they were short of water because Lytchett was not on the mains. Jock saw a plane flying low, probably to check out soldiers camped in the woods, and cried out 'It's a German' but the children avoided being strafed.[28]

For reasons unknown, Alicia was very eager to outlive her husband. They were virtually the same age. Evelyn died on 1st April 1941 at Lytchett and was buried at the family's private chapel (now St Aldhelm's Church) on 5th April.

Although she had given up her charitable work with the Society for the Overseas Settlement of British Women when she became ill in 1938, Alicia remained on the Management Board of Chelsea Physic Garden. She presented several gifts during 1939–40, resigning on 12th June 1941, the year the garden was bombed with incendiaries, owing to an 'inability to attend future meetings of the committee because of removal to the country'.[29] At this meeting the Clerk was able to report two further gifts: a box of timber specimens from the Federated Malay

States and a painting in oils of *Amherstia nobilis*, which she saw as her own 'family tree'. It was very much admired by the Committee whose members read out her notes on its history:

The *Amherstia nobilis* was discovered by Wallich in Burma in 1827 growing (not wild) near a monastery. He named it after Lord Amherst, then Governor of India. There was great excitement when a plant was sent to the Duke of Devonshire, and Paxton built the great house for it at Chatsworth. But another tree sent to Mrs Lawrence (mother of Sir Trevor) was first to flower in 1837. Both trees eventually died. I can remember being taken as a child to Kew to see one there, a tall, lanky tree, which had never flowered. Shortly after a plant was sent to Kew, and as there was no suitable place for it, it was given to my father, the first Lord Amherst of Hackney. He built a house for it, and in 1887 he sent the first beautiful flower to Queen Victoria. It flowered beautifully every year, and I painted this in January 1890 or '91, when it had 50 blooms … The tree died in 1906. Lord Amherst had it in his study, and after his death in 1909 my own painting of the family tree was given to me.

Alicia remained at Lytchett, surrounded by her family, sitting out under the cedar on the West Lawn and reading tales such as *Little Lord Fauntleroy* to her grandchildren, disposing property as gifts and dictating autobiographical notes. Of Chelsea Physic Garden she wrote: 'It has been a great interest and joy all my life …' but curiously, 'I had really forgotten many of my gardening doings until I was tearing up letters, lately.'[30] This was probably because from her mid-fifties onwards she was intensely involved with the emigration societies and with being the wife of a politician.

Alicia died on 14th September 1941, less than six months after her husband, and was buried beside him. Her obituary in *The Times* of 15th September, however, remembers her not for emigration or politics but as 'The Dowager Lady Rockley, writer on Gardening'.[31]

Epilogue

Perhaps the saddest thing in Alicia's life (and which might well have been responsible for her long illness) was the loss of her old home at Didlington. During the Second World War, the house became the HQ of the 7th Armoured Division ('The Desert Rats') under General Dempsey prior to the Normandy landings, with direct phone links to the War Office. By the time of Alicia's death it was still the property of Colonel Smith, who had enlarged it and made the grounds famous in cricketing circles. But the story was not happy. The Colonel's daughter, Ruby, had married an ex-Luftwaffe pilot by the name of Zeitler and been promptly disinherited by her father – as was her brother who had returned from war with decidedly socialist ideas, then married and gone to live in America. Colonel Smith died in 1948, having refused to sell the house he loved, despite it being difficult to obtain staff and run such a place after the war. Ruby's husband also died in 1948 whereupon she decided to return to the place she too loved and bought the old laundry. Then, tragically, the second 'Deluge' occurred. She wrote in a letter, dated May 1983:

> [To buy the laundry was] The worst mistake I ever made. As the beauty I so loved was destroyed by the speculator before my eyes. This need never have happened & was again due to a crooked agent. The settling of my father's affairs was left in the hands of two nephews who had no experience in such matters, & the agent who wanted to keep a slice of it for himself, persuaded them that it was best to split the place up as it would never go as a whole. Not true. John D. Wood, one of the largest estate agents in England, told me they had more than one buyer interested in the whole. Unfortunately they listened to the Agent. A local timber merchant bought all the wonderful trees, & another the house where several sales were held for the fittings, fitments, lovely panelling, unique fireplaces etc.[1]

The auction, by the firm of Curtis and Henson, took place in Didling-ton's ballroom on 6th October 1949. The Hall was finally demolished in 1950, like so many grand pre-war houses.

On a happier note, the Didlington site with 150 acres, including 50 of woodland, was purchased in January 1993 by Elizabeth Orr Sutcliffe and Fiona Dixon. At the time they knew nothing of the history of the estate but have since accumulated a comprehensive archive. A six-bedroomed manor house has now been erected on the site of the old hall with architectural references to the Egyptian interests of the Amherst family. The estate is to be put into a charitable trust. The old kitchen garden has been run since 1963 as a successful retail nursery, Didlington Nurseries, although the glasshouses (including the *Amherstia* house) have been pulled down. Of the main garden there are remains of Alicia's rock garden, the boat houses, Italianate swimming pool and the Castle Cave – and everywhere are trees, the lakes Alicia enjoyed and the lovely Norfolk light.

Lytchett Heath became a convalescent home during the Second World War. Alicia's grandson, Lord James Rockley, maintained Alicia's passion for the woodland garden which he replanted with an interesting rhododendron collection. A huge *Rosa banksiae* replaces the *Magnolia grandiflora* on the South Front which now faces onto lawns rather than Italianate parterres, but continues to house tender plants such as *Cistus*. The vast acreage of *Erica*, which tempted visits by successive Directors of Kew, has been reduced because of the fire risk, but the garden is otherwise much as Alicia would have known it with its splendid conifers.

Alicia outlived her sister, Sib. A fluent linguist in French, German, Italian, Russian, Flemish and Arabic, she had served as an interpreter in the 1914–18 War on a destroyer, while Alicia was busy at the Food Department, but had contracted an illness in Flanders which gave her acute arthritis and she died in 1926. Maggie was already dead (1923). However, Flo outlived Alicia and had an interesting, unmarried life, starting the Egg Marketing scheme in Norfolk known as 'Rose Eggs' and breeding and showing white Arabian pigeons and Embden geese. She became President of the National Poultry Organisation and the first importer of Saluki dogs into Britain. Like Alicia, she wrote on garden-ing: in 1902 *The Book of Town and Window Gardening* and in 1911 *The Herb*

Garden (both published by Frances A. Bardswell). She died at Lytchett Heath[2] in 1946.

Of Alicia's children, Robert William Evelyn Cecil became the Second Baron Rockley and died in 1976, leaving Lytchett Heath to his son James though, since 2008, it has been occupied by James' son Tony. Margaret Gertrude married Captain Herbert Lane on 7th February 1929 and died in 1962. Maud Katherine Alicia, her youngest daughter, was a portrait artist in her own right. She died in 1981, leaving a daughter, Oriel, who married an expert in Persian antiquities. Their daughter is now a Senior Curator at the Victoria and Albert Museum and is named Alicia after her grandmother.

The current Amherst title is held by William, son of William Hugh Amherst Cecil, Fourth Baron Amherst, great grandson of Alicia's eldest sister, May who had kept up the Amherst interest in sailing at Lymington, Hampshire and died in 2009. Their one-time holiday home, Lou Casteou, remains, imposing amid its woodland estate inland from San Raphael and has recently changed hands.

As to Alicia's literary output, it is strangely neglected, especially given the dearth of published material on gardening in the medieval period. All her books are out of print and there has been no attempt to produce facsimile reprints – in contrast to Gertrude Jekyll's literary legacy. Unlike Gertrude Jekyll or Ellen Willmott she has had, until now, no biography. In part, this may be because her publications appeared under different names. She never seems to have considered using a pen name. Nowadays, this would be termed a lack of awareness of 'brand'. As the late, well-respected, botanist and librarian Professor William Stearn wrote, 'Gardeners complain about the difficulties made for them by botanists through changes in the nomenclature of plants, as she did, but never spare any sympathy for the perplexed librarians and cataloguers who find eventually that the Hon. Alicia Amherst, the Hon. Mrs Evelyn Cecil, the Lady Rockley of Lytchett Heath and the Dowager Baroness Rockley were one and the same author.'[3]

However, today there is a garden history movement which would have delighted her. There is a new initiative by the Royal Horticultural Society to get all children gardening, and many integrated horticultural colleges find that they have more female than male students. Britain's empire has been relinquished but emigration remains strong. In

Swaffham, the town museum has opened a room dedicated to local boy made good, Howard Carter, and has an archive of materials relating to the Amhersts at Didlington. And at the Royal Botanic Gardens, Kew, there is one specimen of *Amherstia nobilis* – in the Palm House.

Notes

Chapter 1

1. *Notes on my life and family for my children*, dated 19th January 1908. Manuscript held at Lytchett Heath in the possession of the present Lord Rockley.
2. They had come from the Temple of Mut at Karnak. See: 'Statues of the Goddess Sekhmet' by Albert M. Lythgoe in *Bulletin of the Metropolitan Museum of Art*, October 1919, Supplement.
3. 'The Didlington Hall Estate and its owner', in *Norfolk Chronicle*, 21st November 1885.
4. James Veitch of Chelsea provided, on 20th February 1897, *Bambusa tessel-lata* and *Phyllostachys mitis, juiliosi, henonis, aurea, kumasasa* and *nitida*. William Robinson is also recorded as having despatched plants to her in October 1894, from his house at 63, Lincoln's Inn Fields [Amherst Archive, Chelsea Physic Garden].
5. *Notes on my life* …, op. cit.
6. Ibid.
7. Ibid.
8. *Odd Notes by Alicia Margaret Cecil (née Amherst) Great Granny's sister*. A type-script kept at Didlington in the possession of Elizabeth Orr Sutcliffe.
9. Ibid. The doll she mentions here may have been the one she called 'Robert Cecil'. Curiously, Alicia was to marry Evelyn Cecil and bore him a son she named Robert. Her grand-daughter, Oriel Robinson, maintains that this and other instances indicate she was psychic. Her father, like many Victorians, was interested in the occult. However, when writing of her illness of 1908–14, Alicia claimed, 'It is lucky the future is hidden!' (*Notes on my life* …, op. cit.).
10. *Notes on my life* …, op. cit.
11. A full description of the garden at Didlington Hall is given in James William Trimbee's *Memories of Didlington Hall* in the Norfolk County

Records Office, Amherst Collection: MC82/1, 522x5. James Trimbee was Second Journeyman in the greenhouse from February 1902. He nearly poisoned the Duchess of Saxe-Coburg and her daughter by applying a fertiliser to the dessert strawberries, which turned out to be human waste. The tainted fruit was promptly boiled for jam and he was transferred to raising the late flowering chrysanthemums for which Didlington became famous during the autumn shooting season.

Chapter 2

1. The description of Didlington Hall is from *Didlington Hall* by Cracknell, a catalogue published at the Express Printing Works, Cambridge and now in the Norwich County Records Office: MC84/168.
2. Cecil, The Hon. Mrs Evelyn, *A History of Gardening in England*, 3rd edn (London: John Murray, 1910), Preface.
3. Amherst Archive, Chelsea Physic Garden: Box A.
4. Ibid.
5. *Odd Notes …*, op. cit.
6. Ibid.
7. Ibid.
8. Lindley named this plant *Victoria regia*, the name favoured in most botanical circles rather than Schomburgh's '*Victoria Regina*'. Today it is called *Victoria amazonica* after the river where it occurs.
9. Ibid.
10. Ibid.
11. Ibid.
12. Ibid.
13. Ibid.
14. Ibid.
15. Article entitled 'The Garden', of 7th November 1891 in the Hackney Archives Department of the National Archive.
16. *Odd Notes …*, op. cit.
17. Ibid.
18. Ibid.

Chapter 3

1. Lady Amherst of Hackney, *A sketch of Egyptian History from the earliest time to the present day* (London: Methuen & Co., 1904). According to Howard Carter's biographer, T.G.H. James, this was considered an interesting account suitable for a general readership and was well received.
2. Amherst Archive, Chelsea Physic Garden.

3. James, T.G.H., *Howard Carter: the path to Tutankhamun* (London: Tauris Parke Paperbacks, 2006) p. 11.
4. Amherst Archive, Chelsea Physic Garden: Box C gives the later date. The Newberry Collection, Griffith Institute, University of Oxford, mentions Carter arranging the collection on 10th November 1892.
5. Norfolk County Records Office, Amherst Collection: M84, p. 31.
6. Griffith Institute, Newberry MSS 1. 2/48-70.
7. Ibid. MSS 1. 2/71-101.
8. James, *Howard Carter*, op. cit., p. 37.
9. Quoted in Skipper, Keith, *Hidden Norfolk* (Newbury: Countryside Books, 1998).
10. I am indebted to Venetia Chattey (grand-daughter of Alicia's sister, Margaret) for the permission to quote from the first and second volumes of *Didlington up the Nile*.
11. Griffith Institute, Newberry MSS 1. 1/23-64; 17th April 1895. Percy Newberry married Essie Johnston on 12th February 1907. She donated his correspondence to the Griffith Institute in 1950 after his death in 1949.

Chapter 4

1. Griffith Institute, Newberry MSS 1. 1/23-64.
2. *The Academy*, 7th March 1896.
3. *The Spectator*, 2nd May 1896.
4. *Economic Review*, April 1896.
5. Amherst Archive, Chelsea Physic Garden – annotated press cutting: 'This review I believe was by Miss Gertrude Jekyll who died about 85 in 1931–2.'
6. 'We agree heartily with Miss Amherst when she writes that, we should be thankful indeed that "a few people were left of sufficient strength of mind to resist the all-powerful Brown".' (*Quarterly Review*, July 1896).
7. This is made clear in *Gertrude Jekyll, a memoir* by her nephew, Francis Jekyll (London: Jonathan Cape, 1934), p. 166.
8. *Odd Notes* …, op. cit. Alicia used several different publishers in her lifetime and sometimes took advice on how to get the best terms and distribution; [e.g. Letter to R.E. Prothero, 22nd February 1900, who recommended Murray for best terms and 'has travellers' (i.e. salesmen). Amherst Archive, Chelsea Physic Garden: Box A].
9. The only other contender was George W. Johnson's *History of English Gardening* (London, 1829).
10. Amherst Archive, Chelsea Physic Garden.

11. *A History of Gardening in England*, 3rd edn, op. cit., Preface.
12. Amherst Archive, Chelsea Physic Garden: Box B.
13. Amherst Archive, Chelsea Physic Garden: Box C.
14. Successive scholars used her bibliography; e.g. Eleanor Sinclair Rohde enquired on 14th June 1922, for an English translation of the herbalist Macer. Organisations, too, often approached her for her opinion; e.g. in March 1914 the Royal Society of Arts approached her for comments on Indian water gardens to follow a paper to be read by Mr Patrick Villiers-Stuart. Her response was sensible: knowing she had never 'been much further East than Aden' she counselled against a style being adopted 'simply because its [sic] the fashion'. Rather, a new garden for Dehli should either 'fulfill the old Indian ideal, or should be a new style evolved from England and adapted to the Indian climate' [Amherst Archive, Chelsea Physic Garden].
15. She had sent the proofs of *The History* to be checked by Baker [Amherst Archive, Chelsea Physic Garden: Box B].
16. *Odd Notes ...*, op. cit. Her grandson James, Lord Rockley, later married the daughter of Earl Cadogan, Lady Sarah Cadogan, so maintaining the link with the Cadogan family.

Chapter 5
1. The Women's Library of the London Metropolitan Archive contains much on this issue.
2. Amherst Archive, Chelsea Physic Garden: Box B. Lady Warwick was more successful than Swanley who had tried in January 1898 to get Alicia onto the Committee of their Women's Branch. The Lady Warwick Hostel became the all-female Studley College in 1910.
3. Ibid.
4. *A History of Gardening in England*, 3rd edn, op. cit., p. 314.
5. Amherst Archive, Chelsea Physic Garden: Box B.
6. Ibid.
7. Amherst Archive, Chelsea Physic Garden: Box A.
8. Amherst Archive, Chelsea Physic Garden: Box B – proof of an article dated 13th April 1912: 'Affectation in Gardening', published in the *National Review* (expanded from an original article dated 20th May 1898).
9. *Odd Notes ...*, op. cit.

Chapter 6
1. Report in the *Thetford and Watton Times*, 19th February 1898.
2. Amherst Archive, Chelsea Physic Garden: Box C. There is also a list of

'Ideas for Quarterly Article' in Box A, with drafts of same.

3. *Notes on my life …*, op. cit.

4. *Odd Notes …*, op. cit.

5. *A History of Gardening in England*, 3rd edn, op. cit., p. 311. Alicia always had immense respect for Kew: 'Next time you visit Kew think of the brains and the skill required to direct and carry on its many sided activities, economic and scientific, and at the same time to enhance its beauty and maintain that dignity and spacious calm which makes the Royal Gardens, Kew, unique among the botanical institutions of the world' ['The Royal Gardens, Kew' in *The Listener*, 29th April 1936].

6. Royal Botanic Gardens, Kew, *Directors' Correspondence*: DC193, No. 18.

7. Amherst Archive, Chelsea Physic Garden.

8. *Odd Notes …*, op. cit.

9. Cecil, The Hon. Mrs Evelyn, *Children's Gardens* (London and New York: Macmillan & Co., 1903), Preface.

10. Ibid. p. 33.

11. Ibid. p. 77.

12. Ibid. p. 160.

13. Jekyll, Gertrude, *Children and Gardens* (London: Country Life, 1908), p. 25.

14. Ibid. p. 146. Ellen Willmott offered Alicia advice on *Children's Gardens*: 'I would draw some ideal children's gardens which would illustrate your remarks & then the sketches could be reproduced by a process & if coloured would make a capital frontispiece.' But this advice does not appear to have been followed. [Letter sent from Bishopstowe, Torquay, dated 24th January 1902. Chelsea Physic Garden, Amherst Archive: Box B.]

15. Amherst Archive, Chelsea Physic Garden.

16. *The Morning Advertiser*, 22nd December 1902.

17. *Odd Notes …*, op. cit.

18. Cecil, The Hon. Mrs Evelyn, *London Parks and Gardens* (London: Archibald Constable & Co., 1907), p. 30.

19. Ibid. pp. 20–1.

20. Ibid. p. 121.

21. Ibid. pp. 99–100.

22. Amherst Archive, Chelsea Physic Garden: Box B. Details of a chrysanthemum exhibition at Stoke Newington, 10th and 11th November 1897, and a talk on 'The Chrysanthemum', annotated: 'I think this was at a show in the Shoreditch Town Hall – ?1894? I really cannot remember. A.M.C. 1933.'

23. *London Parks and Gardens*, op. cit., p. 160.

24. Ibid. p. 129.
25. Ibid. p. 218.
26. Ibid. pp. 215–6.
27. Ibid. p. 346.
28. Ibid. pp. 327–8.
29. Amherst Archive, Chelsea Physic Garden: Box B. Redesdale letter, 13th April 1907.

Chapter 7

1. *Odd Notes …*, op. cit.
2. Archives of the Women's Library, London Metropolitan Archive. South African Expansion Committee: Letters to the Johannesburg Committee, 1902–4 [Box FLO 41 (1/SAX/3/1 & 2)].
3. Ibid. Letters to Lady Maud Selborne, 25th May 1906.
4. Ibid. Report of SACS 1903, pp. 73–4.
5. Ibid. Letter to Miss Russell, 31st October 1902.
6. Wallach, Janet, *Desert Queen: The Extraordinary Life of Gertrude Bell, adventurer, adviser to kings, ally of Lawrence of Arabia* (London: Weidenfeld & Nicolson, 1996).
7. I am grateful to Brian Duggan (*Saluki International*, Spring/Summer 1994, pp. 50–9) for this information.
8. *Odd Notes …*, op. cit.
9. *Minutes of the Chelsea Physic Garden Management Council*, Chelsea Physic Garden.
10. Minter, Sue, *The Apothecaries' Garden: a history of the Chelsea Physic Garden*, Chapter 5 (Stroud: Sutton Publishing, 2000).
11. *Minutes of the Chelsea Physic Garden …*, op. cit., 30th June 1904. The Committee was 'staggered at the cost': Letter from H. Howard Batten [Amherst Archive, Chelsea Physic Garden: Box B].
12. *Minutes of the Chelsea Physic Garden …*, op. cit., Minute 158.
13. Ibid. Minute 157.
14. Ibid. Minute 168.
15. Minter, Sue, *The Apothecaries' Garden …*, op. cit., p. 90. All Alicia's publications were donated to, and remain in, the library at Chelsea Physic Garden.
16. *Minutes of the Chelsea Physic Garden …*, op. cit., Minute 159.
17. Ibid. Minute 356.
18. Ibid. Minute 561.
19. Amherst Archive, Chelsea Physic Garden: Box B.

20. *Minutes of the Chelsea Physic Garden* …, op. cit., Minute Nos 226, 508, 984 and 1015.
21. *Minutes of the Chelsea Physic Garden* …, op. cit., 13th June 1941.
22. *Odd Notes* …, op. cit. She describes the growth of the Garden City movement in the *History*, 3rd edn, p. 315. Barnett is also listed as giving a talk on 'The Garden Suburb' at the Country in Town Exhibition, 6th July 1906 [Amherst Archive, Chelsea Physic Garden].
23. Ibid.
24. Ibid.
25. *Notes on my life* …, op. cit.

Chapter 8

1. Amherst, Alicia, *Journal* (1897), 'Valescure – Aix-les-Bains'. I am grateful to Venetia Chattey for sight of these two small volumes from which these extracts are taken.
2. Griffith Institute, Newberry MSS 1, 2/71-101.
3. Hackney Archives, Amherst Collection: section Valescure, where there are also architect's plans.
4. *Notes on my life* …, op. cit.
5. Hackney Archives, op. cit., Letter from J. Mitford in Northumberland, 20th June 1906 [D/F/AMH/13/471].
6. Griffith Institute, Newberry MSS 1 9/1-29, Carter.
7. *Notes on my life* …, op. cit.
8. Griffith Institute, Newberry MSS 1 2/1-47.
9. Ibid. MSS 1 1/23-64.
10. Ibid. MSS 1 2/48-70.
11. Norfolk County Records Office, Amherst Collection, MC84, p. 37.
12. Amherst Archive, Chelsea Physic Garden: Letters from D.W. Prowe (?), 27th March 1907, and Lord Redesdale, 7th October 1906. The only book to escape the sale was the 15th century *Of the Imitation of Christ* by St Thomas à Kempis, a meditation on the life and teaching of Jesus, which provided Lord Amherst some comfort. It had been with him in France when 'The Deluge' broke.
13. Trimbee, James William, *Memories of Didlington Hall*, Norfolk County Records Office, Amherst Collection: MC82/1. He noted that there were other instances of abuse of the Amherst's good nature – e.g. alcoholism among the servants, following the free supply of beer in the Butler's Pantry.
14. Hackney Archives, op. cit. – unattributed and undated obituary of Lord Amherst.

15. Ibid.
16. Ibid.
17. *Odd Notes …*, op. cit.

Chapter 9

1. Amherst Archive, Chelsea Physic Garden.
2. I am indebted to Dr Arthur Hollman, retired cardiologist and one time Advisor for the Royal College of Physicians to the Chelsea Physic Garden, for this information.
3. In *Notes on my life …* she describes her state of mind 18 months after 'The Deluge': '[having] to face a new state of things, one never felt certain of anything, and this sense of insecurity is ever present.'
4. *Odd Notes …*, op. cit. A total of around 100,000 women worked as professional or voluntary nurses in the Great War. In Norwich County Records, Amherst Collection: MC 84/204 528x1, there are 79 photographs of the Amherst sisters nursing at the Auxiliary Hospital.
5. National Archives, Kew: MAF 42/14.
6. Ibid.
7. *Odd Notes …*, op. cit. The Women's Institutes were the bodies the Board of Education used to arrange collection of 'The Wild Fruit Crop'. They also arranged for the collection of 'leaves and roots of common wild plants' for pharmaceutical use. See: Memoranda Nos 25 and 27, 'The Schools in War Time' (Board of Education). I am indebted to Anne Grikitis for this information.
8. Reminiscences of Oriel Robinson given orally to the author.
9. *Notes on my life …*, op. cit. There is undated evidence ('Notes for the children's book on foods, etc') that Alicia was hoping for another book from her work on food, but this never materialised [Amherst Archive, Chelsea Physic Garden: Box B].

Chapter 10

1. Cecil CBE, The Hon. Lady, 'Lytchett Heath Garden' in *RHS Journal, 1931*, pp. 56–60. The species named are as Alicia wrote them; there have been some changes in nomenclature since. For example, *Cedrus atlantica* would now be *Cedrus libani* or *Cedrus libani* ssp. *atlantica*.
2. Ibid. This article contains a picture of her and Evelyn with their heads just showing above the *Erica*.
3. Royal Botanic Gardens, Kew, *Directors' Correspondence*: DC 107, No. 248.
4. Ibid. DC 107, No. 250.
5. Ibid. DC 107, No. 249.

6. 'Lytchett Heath Garden', op. cit.
7. Letter dated 21st October 1900, sent to Lytchett Heath [Amherst Archive, Chelsea Physic Garden: Box B].
8. Royal Botanic Gardens, Kew, *Directors' Correspondence*: Vol. 119, English Letters, Barr-Cro 1911–1920.
9. 'Lytchett Heath Garden', op. cit.
10. I am indebted to Oriel Robinson for her memories of this as a child. She remembers red, black and white currants in the fruit cage and both red and green gooseberries. Also, that on the wall below the lawn Alicia grew sun-loving plants and pointed out a gentian to Oriel which she said was not at all easy to grow. There were masses of wood anemones in the woods, and celandines too.
11. Royal Botanic Gardens, Kew, *Directors' Correspondence*: Vol. 125, No. 388. The timber negatives are now in the Norfolk County Records Office.

Chapter 11

1. A full account of the Saqqara incident and subsequent events is given in James, T.G.H., *Howard Carter: the path to Tutankhamun* (London: Tauris Parke Paperbacks, 2006) pp. 114ff.
2. Griffith Institute, Newberry MSS 1. 2/1-47.
3. *Howard Carter ...*, op. cit., p. 240.
4. I am grateful to The Hon. Angela Reid for this suggestion.
5. *Howard Carter*, op. cit., p. 240.
6. Ibid. p. 250.
7. Griffith Institute, Newberry MSS 1. 8/60-83.
8. Ibid.
9. *Howard Carter*, op. cit., pp. 433–4.
10. Napoleon's army had discovered many antiquities in Egypt which had inspired much popular interest in the ancient civilisation and the Rosetta Stone (which provided the key to deciphering hieroglyphics), when brought to the British Museum in 1802, initiated a passion for studying inscriptions.
11. Griffith Institute, Newberry MSS 1. 1/23-64.

Chapter 12

1. Royal Botanic Gardens, Kew, *Directors' Correspondence*: Vol. 125, No. 389.
2. Rockley, Lady, *Wild Flowers of the Great Dominions of the British Empire*, (London: Macmillan & Co., 1935).
3. Ibid. p. 38.
4. Royal Botanic Gardens, Kew, *Directors' Correspondence*: Vol. 25, No. 392.

5. Ibid.
6. Ibid. p. 196.
7. Ibid. pp. 147–8 ('Tanglefoot' is *Bauera rubioides*).
8. Ibid. p. 151.
9. Ibid. p .154.
10. *Wild Flowers* ..., op. cit., pp. 78 and 86.
11. Ibid. p. 84.
12. Ibid. p. 82.
13. Ibid. p. 127.
14. Ibid. p. 133.
15. Ibid. p. 139.
16. Ibid. p. 104.
17. Ibid. p. 118. *Duboisia* has been cultivated in Australia as a source of hyoscine, important in the pharmaceutical industry for treating nausea and motion sickness and as an anticholinergic drug in anaesthetic pre-medication.
18. Ibid. p. 156.
19. Ibid. p. 105.
20. Ibid. p. 166. Named in *Kew Bulletin*, No. 7, 1934.
21. Ibid. pp. 166–7.
22. Ibid. p. 175.

Chapter 13

1. *Journal of Botany*, September 1935, Vol. LXXIII, pp. 268–9. The reviewer was 'A.B.R.'.
2. *Wild Flowers* ..., op. cit., pp. 236–7.
3. Ibid. pp. 293–4.
4. Ibid. p. 243.
5. Ibid. pp. 248 and 253.
6. Ibid. p. 261.
7. Ibid. p. 264.
8. Ibid. p. 283.
9. Ibid. p. 285
10. Ibid. p. 289.
11. Ibid. p. 291.
12. Ibid. p. 293.
13. Ibid. p. 294.
14. Ibid. p. 296.
15. Ibid. p. 316.
16. Ibid. p. 318.

17. Ibid. p. 336.
18. Ibid. p. 340.
19. Ibid. pp. 344–5.
20. Ibid.
21. *Kew Bulletin*, No. 5, 1935, pp. 338–9.
22. Rockley, Lady, *Historic Gardens of England* (London: Country Life, 1938), p. 32.
23. Ibid. pp. 32, 33 and 35.
24. Ibid. pp. 45 and 47.
25. Ibid. pp. 51 and 53.
26. Ibid. p. 58.
27. Ibid. p. 130.
28. The reminiscences of Oriel Robinson, Alicia's grand-daughter, include further memories of Mrs Holbrook as a large lady who cooked for them all (with some assistance), and of Swiss governesses. The youngest three grandchildren had a nanny, ate upstairs and later moved away from Lytchett Heath. As an Army Brigade HQ it was home to camouflaged soldiers camping in the woods and officers billeted in the rear quarters of the house. Evacuees were also moved in shortly after the start of the war but did not stay long. Oriel was told they did not like the sound of wind in the trees!
29. *Minutes of the City Parochial Foundation*, Chelsea Physic Garden Library.
30. *Odd Notes ...*, op. cit.
31. Biography pamphlets in the Library, Royal Botanic Gardens, Kew.

Epilogue

1. Letter from Ruby Zeitler to Mrs McKenzie dated 11th May 1983, in the ownership of Elizabeth Orr Sutcliffe at Didlington Manor. Though noting that agents were again to be the ruin of the Didlington Estate, she rebuts the local rumours that the ill luck was due to Tutankhamun's curse. Locals said (incorrectly) that one of Didlington's mummies had been sold to an American who took it home on the *Titanic*.
2. Notes from Cherry Strange, kept at Didlington Manor in the possession of Elizabeth Orr Sutcliffe.
3. *Journal of Garden History*, Vol. 5 (1), 1977–8.

Bibliography

Manuscript Sources

Alicia Amherst Archive, Chelsea Physic Garden, London.

The family archive of The Hon. Angela Reid, Dorchester-on-Thames, Oxon. and her online archive www.amhersts-of-didlington.com

Minutes of the City Parochial Foundation, Chelsea Physic Garden.

The Didlington Archive of Elizabeth Orr Sutcliffe and Fiona Dixon, Didlington Manor, Norfolk.

Didlington up the Nile: the Journal of Alicia M.J. Amherst, Dec. 1894 to June 1895, Vol. 1. In the possession of Venetia Chattey.

Howard Carter and Percy Newberry Papers, The Griffith Institute, University of Oxford.

The Hackney Archives Department of the Natonal Archives.

The National Archives, Kew, Richmond, Surrey.

Norfolk County Records Office, Norwich.

The family archive of Oriel Robinson.

The family archive of Lord Rockley, Lytchett Heath, Poole, Dorset.

Directors' Correspondence, Library of the Royal Botanic Gardens, Kew.

The Howard Carter Archive, Swaffham Museum, Swaffham, Norfolk.

The Women's Library, London Metropolitan Archive.

Newspaper References

Thetford & Watton Times, 8th February 1896 (Review of *A History of Gardening in England*).

Thetford & Watton Times, 4th September 1897 (Jubilee festivities at Didlington Hall).

Thetford & Watton Times, 19th February 1898 (Report of marriage of Alicia Amherst to Mr Evelyn Cecil).

Daily Telegraph, 12th August 1992 (Pocock, Tom, 'When the Nile Came to Norfolk').

Works by Alicia Amherst

As Alicia Amherst

'A Fifteenth Century Treatise on Gardening by Mayster Ion Gardener' in *Archaeologia*, Vol. LIV, 1894.

A History of Gardening in England (London: Bernard Quaritch, 1895).

A History of Gardening in England, 2nd edn (London: Bernard Quaritch, 1896).

As The Hon. Mrs Evelyn Cecil

Children's Gardens (London & New York: Macmillan & Co., 1903).

London Parks and Gardens (London: Archibald Constable & Co., 1907).

'Alpine Flowers at Home' in *National Review*, No. 304, June 1908.

A History of Gardening in England, 3rd edn (London: John Murray, 1910).

'Substance and Shadow', No. 38 (London: National League for Opposing Woman Suffrage, 1910?).

As The Hon. Lady Cecil, CBE

'The Garden at Lytchett Heath, Dorsetshire' in *RHS Journal*, 1931, pp. 56–60.

As Lady Rockley

'Plant Names History in Names' in *The Gardener's Year Book*, 1929, edited by G.J.H. Moultrey Read.

Wild Flowers of the Great Dominions of the British Empire (London: Macmillan & Co., 1935).

'The Royal Gardens, Kew', in *The Listener*, 29th April 1936.

Some Canadian Wildflowers (Toronto: Macmillan Company of Canada, 1937).

Historic Gardens of England (London: Country Life, 1938 & New York: Charles Scribner's Sons, 1938).

Works by Margaret, Lady Amherst

Amherst, Lady Margaret, *A Sketch of Egyptian History from the earliest time to the present day* (London: Methuen & Co., 1904).

Periodicals

'The Didlington Hall Estate and its owners' in *Norfolk Chronicle*, 21st November 1885.

Lythgoe, Albert M., 'Statues of the Goddess Sekhmet' in *Bulletin of the Metropolitan Museum of Art*, Supplement, October 1919, pp. 3–22.

Review of 'Wild Flowers of the Great Dominions of the British Empire' in *Journal of Botany*, September 1935, LXXIII, pp. 268–9.

Review of 'Wild Flowers of the Great Dominions of the British Empire' in *Kew Bulletin*, No. 5, 1935, pp. 338–9.

Stearn, Professor William, 'Alicia Amherst' in *Garden History*, Vol. 5 (1), 1977–8.

Percy, Joan, 'Author by Accident' in *The Garden*, March 1989.

Ikin, Ed, 'Alicia Amherst', *Newsletter of The Friends of Chelsea Physic Garden*, Spring/Summer 2003, pp. 22–3.

Harrison, Lorraine, 'Ladies in Bloomers' in *Gardens Illustrated*, December 2005, pp. 64–9.

Colquhoun, Kate, 'Paxton's nemesis' in *The Garden*, Vol. 131, Part 1, January 2006, pp. 26–7 [on *Amherstia nobilis*].

Secondary Sources

Jekyll, Gertrude, *Children and Gardens* (London: Country Life, 1908).

Le Lièvre, Audrey, *Miss Willmott of Warley Place* (London: Faber, 1980).

Massingham, Betty, *A Century of Gardeners* (London: Faber, 1982).

Brown, Jane, *Eminent Gardeners: some people of influence and their gardens, 1880–1980* (London & New York: Viking, 1990).

Kellaway, Deborah (ed.), *The Illustrated Virago Book of Women Gardeners* (London: Virago Press, 1997).

Skipper, Keith, *Hidden Norfolk* (Newbury: Countryside Books, 1998).

James, T.G.H., *Howard Carter: the path to Tutankhamun* (London: Tauris Parke Paperbacks, 2006).

Winstone, H.V.F., *Howard Carter and the discovery of the tomb of Tutankhamun*, revised edn (Manchester: Barzan Publishing, 2006).

Ikin, Ed, *Historian, Gardener and Botanist: an appraisal of the Life and Work of Alicia Amherst* [Dissertation for MA in Garden History, Birkbeck College, University of London – unpublished].

Index

121

INDEX